Ninja® Foodi™ Cold & Hot Blender
COOKBOOK FOR BEGINNERS

Made in the USA
Coppell, TX
21 February 2021

NINJA® Foodi™

COLD & HOT BLENDER

COOKBOOK FOR BEGINNERS

100 RECIPES FOR SMOOTHIES, SOUPS, INFUSED COCKTAILS, SAUCES, AND MORE

Kenzie Swanhart

ROCKRIDGE PRESS

For general information on our other products and services or to obtain technical support, please contact our Customer Care Department within the U.S. at (866) 744-2665, or outside the U.S. at (510) 253-0500.

Rockridge Press publishes its books in a variety of electronic and print formats. Some content that appears in print may not be available in electronic books, and vice versa.

Interior and Cover Designer: Liz Cosgrove
Art Producer: Karen Beard
Editor: Salwa Jabado
Production Editor: Andrew Yackira
Production Manager: Jose Olivera
Photography: ©2019 Hélène Dujardin, food styling by Tami Hardeman, except pp. 40, 44, 46, 72, 76, 78, 80, 82, 124, 126, 128, 152, 160, 162, 164, 166, 182, & 190 ©Stocksy; pp. 36, 184, & 188 © Shutterstock; pg. 34 © Linda Schneider; pp. 42 & 110 © Darren Muir; pg. 52 © iStock; pg. 112 © Nadine Greeff; pg.114 © Marija Vidal & pg. 120 © Evi Abeler. Author photo courtesy of Julien Levesque.

ISBN: Print 978-1-64611-019-3
eBook 978-1-64611-020-9
R1
Printed in Canada

For Sasha,
thank you for your endless
support and inspiration

CONTENTS

INTRODUCTION

I'M GOING TO LET YOU IN ON A LITTLE SECRET: I LOVE MY JOB.
As the head of the Culinary Innovation and Marketing team at Ninja®, I not only help design and develop products that transform the way you cook, but I also get to write and develop the recipes that allow you to fall in love with our products.

Readers like you are the reason I do what I do. You are the reason my team and I spend countless hours in the Ninja Test Kitchen creating prototypes, building intelligent programs, and evaluating every change made to our products. From increasing the temperature of the heating element, to adding nonstick coatings, down to the number of ingredients in each recipe—no decision is made without thinking about how it will improve your life and your experience in the kitchen.

Over the years, Ninja has transformed the way people blend and prep food with our state-of-the-art blenders, best-in-class single-serve blenders, and space-saving kitchen systems. From the moment I walked in the door, I was blown away by the dedication this company has to delivering 5-star products that improve people's lives every day.

In 2018, we launched the groundbreaking Ninja Foodi™ Pressure Cooker—the pressure cooker that crisps. Combining two powerful technologies, this revolution in cooking took the country by storm. Now, we are bringing a little of that Foodi magic to the blender. Introducing the Ninja Foodi Blender, the blender that cooks. So, you can blend supersmooth smoothies, crush ice for frozen drinks, and cook up sippable smooth soups, slurp-able hearty soups, and delicious creamy sauces.

We know how hard it can be to create healthy meals that tick the boxes of being easy to get on the table—while also tasting great. And even the best cooks among us succumb to the rut of repeating meals multiple times a week due to a sheer lack of time. We've taken all of that into account while bringing this book to life and have

prioritized ease, flavor, and maximizing the many advanced features of the Foodi™.

With the Foodi Blender, you can blend a Tropical Greens Smoothie (page 35), cook up a hearty Banana-Nut Oatmeal (page 49), mix up a White Bean Hummus (page 66), simmer a Simple Swiss Cheese Fondue (page 59), purée a Basil Pesto (page 113), boil a Ginger-Garlic Chicken Ramen (page 93), even crush ice for a Pineapple Margarita (page 138), or whip together a Tiramisu Mousse (page 175). The options are endless.

Consider this book your official guide to the Foodi Blender, packed full of charts and guides to get you started and yummy recipes that will inspire you to cook with your blender over and over again.

1

Ninja® Foodi™ Cold & Hot Blender 101

NINJA® HAS ALWAYS BEEN A PIONEER IN THE SMALL APPLI-
ance industry, providing innovative solutions to help home cooks in
the kitchen. Since launching our first blenders back in 2010, Ninja
continues to push the boundaries and up the blending game: from the
Ninja Master Prep™ blender, that puts the control of blending into the
palm of your hand, to state-of-the-art kitchen systems that combine
full-size blending and food processing into one compact machine.

Now, the Ninja Foodi Blender raises the bar again!

This chapter will introduce you to the blender that crushes—and
cooks. I will break down all of the functions and benefits of the
Ninja Foodi Blender so you can unleash its full potential and
easily whip up delicious meals, snacks, and drinks in an entirely
novel way.

SO MUCH MORE THAN A BLENDER

These days, it seems as if everyone has a blender sitting on their counter collecting dust. Whether you have the hand-me-down your parents passed along when you moved into your first apartment, or that brand-new professional blender from your wedding registry, chances are you don't use your blender for much more than blending your morning smoothie.

Did you know that Ninja® blenders are known for their powerful blades and the ability to crush ice to "snow"? That means that with a powerful Ninja blender you can make frozen drinks and frozen treats in seconds, or liquefy tough fruits and vegetables into juices and smoothies, from a Frozen Sangria (page 141) or Mango Sorbet (page 189) to a Beet and Berry Blast smoothie (page 38).

But what if you could also use your blender to make piping-hot soups and sauces, making mealtime a breeze? With the Foodi™ Blender's precision 800-watt heating element, you can actually cook ingredients and build flavor. Unlike competing blenders that use friction heat to warm ingredients, the Ninja Foodi Blender supplies precise heat and can actually boil liquid in minutes. I'm talking about Creamy Tomato Soup (page 74), Spicy Peanut Sauce (page 108), even Buffalo Chicken Dip (page 70) cooked to perfection in one pitcher!

With the Foodi Blender's precision heating element, you can also infuse natural flavors for craft cocktails, flavored waters, and concentrated mixers. You can create naturally infused spirits in a matter of minutes—versus weeks—such as Cinnamon-Infused Whiskey (page 158) and Lavender-Rosemary Infused Vodka (page 155).

The Ninja Foodi Blender will change your perception of what a blender can do, delivering everything you expect from this kitchen staple, plus so much more! With multiple features at your fingertips, the Foodi will help unlock your creativity and elevate your favorite meals!

Auto iQ

At Ninja®, we redefined blending when we first debuted Auto iQ programs. These intelligent programs leverage a unique set of pulses and pauses to deliver expert blending results at the touch of a button. With the Foodi™ Blender we combine pulsing, pausing, blending, and precision heat!

By controlling both the blending speed and the temperature of the heating element, the Auto iQ programs allow you to make a variety of foods and beverages at the touch of a button—no more guesswork or blender babysitting required. The Foodi Blender offers 11 intelligent Auto iQ program, including:

- SMOOTHIE
- FROZEN DRINK
- EXTRACT
- ICE CREAM
- SAUTÉ
- SAUCE/DIP
- HEARTY SOUP
- SMOOTH SOUP
- MIXER
- WATER
- COCKTAIL

High-Speed Total Crushing

With its powerful blades, the Ninja Foodi Blender has the ability to crush ice and frozen ingredients in seconds for creamy smoothies and resort-style frozen drinks.

Nutrient Extraction

When we debuted the Nutri Ninja™ line, you could only liquefy whole fruits and vegetables for healthy nutrient extractions in our single-serve cups. With the Foodi Blender, you are able to make nutrient extractions in a full-size pitcher and blend up whole-food juices for the whole family!

Precision Heat

What sets the Ninja® Foodi™ Blender apart from all other blenders is the 800-watt precision heating element that boils liquid in minutes. Now you can cook ingredients to unlock their full flavor. Make hearty or smooth soups, simmer flavorful sauces, and even melt chocolate or cheese into fondue.

Rapid Infusion

With the Foodi Blender's precision heating element, you can unlock and rapidly infuse flavors to make spa waters, craft cocktails, and concentrated mixers. The heat is key to breaking down the ingredients.

KNOW YOUR FOODI COMPONENTS

Let's take a look at the various parts and pieces that make up your Foodi Blender. When you're familiar with how the appliance works, you'll be able to start cooking with it that much quicker!

Glass Pitcher

The premium, 64-ounce glass pitcher is the perfect size for blending smoothies and soups for a family of four or puréeing dips and sauces for a crowd. Plus, the nonstick surface makes cleanup a snap. A word of caution: Only use silicone or wooden utensils so you don't scratch the nonstick surface at the bottom of the glass pitcher. To start blending, set the glass pitcher on the base with the Ninja logo facing forward.

Pitcher Lid

The pitcher lid fits securely in place for safe, splash-free blending. To assemble, position the lid tab to the right of the handle and push down. Rotate the lid clockwise so the arrows align. If you remove the lid while blending, the program will automatically pause. Replace the lid and push the program button again to resume where you left off.

Center Cap

Pitcher Lid

Glass Pitcher

High-Speed Crushing Blades

Precision Heating Element

Motor Base

Tamper

Cleaning Brush

Center Cap

Located in the middle of the lid, the center cap doubles as a measuring cup marked with milliliters so you can easily measure ingredients for your favorite recipes. When you want to add ingredients while blending, simply remove the cap and add ingredients through the hole in the center of the pitcher lid.

High-Speed Crushing Blades

The high-speed crushing blades were specifically engineered to crush ice to "snow" and pulverize the toughest ingredients. The blades spin up to 23,000 RPMs, allowing you to make the smoothest smoothies, creamy frozen treats, and even frothy nut milks. Always use caution with the blades! Ninja® has a brush to make cleaning easier, so you don't risk cutting your fingers on the blades.

Precision Heating Element

The Foodi™ Blender is equipped with a precision heating element in its base that adapts to the correct temperature based on the program chosen. With this feature, you can simmer sauces, sauté onions, boil soups, and rapidly infuse flavors into your favorite craft cocktails. While other blenders claim to make soup by heating ingredients via friction, the Foodi Blender's precision heating element actually applies controlled heat to your ingredients, in effect cooking them, and allowing you to build intense flavor.

Motor Base

The powerful motor base houses the motor and the control panel. To clean the motor base, simply press the power button, unplug the unit, and wipe the base clean with a clean, damp cloth.

Tamper

When blending thick ingredients, use the tamper to push the ingredients down toward the blades for supersmooth results. To use, remove the center cap and replace with the tamper. We even built in a scraper tool on the side of the tamper so you can scrape down the sides of the pitcher for thick recipes like ice creams and nut butters.

Cleaning Brush

When handwashing the glass pitcher, use the cleaning brush to safely clean in and around the blades with ease.

KNOW YOUR FOODI™ FUNCTIONS

Now that you are acquainted with the Foodi Blender and its components, let's dive into how it works! Below, I outline the 11 Auto iQ programs that are built into the blender, why it is unique, and what you can look forward to making! I also highlight how to manually cook and blend your favorite recipes if you chose not to use one of the preset programs.

Auto iQ Programs

With our intelligent preset programs, let the Foodi™ Blender do the work!

Smoothie

Blend your favorite fresh or frozen fruits and a splash of milk for delicious, sippable smoothies. Try the Carrot Cake Smoothie (page 39) or the Mango-Berry Protein Smoothie (page 43). Run time: 45 seconds

Extract

Liquefy whole fruits and vegetables for healthy nutrient extractions and whole-food juices. This program is best when using tough, fibrous ingredients like leafy greens, nuts, fruit skins, and seeds. EXTRACT mode is used to make the Tropical Greens Smoothie (page 35) and Creamy Avocado Smoothie (page 37). Run time: 65 seconds

Frozen Drink

Use this mode to crush ice to "snow" for resort-style cocktails and mocktails, like my Frozen Sangria (page 141), Bourbon-Peach Slush (page 143), and Frozen Raspberry Lemonade (page 139). Run time: 55 seconds

Ice Cream

Blend frozen fruits and ice into fresh fruit sorbets, creamy ice cream, and crunchy snow cones. Try the recipes for Blueberry-Buttermilk Ice Cream (page 187), Mango Yogurt Ice Pops (page 191), and Pineapple Whip (page 171). Run time: 70 seconds

Sauté

Many recipes call for you to use the SAUTÉ program as a first step before using another Auto iQ program. This helps to unlock more flavor from aromatic ingredients like onions and garlic before making a soup, sauce, or dip. Run time: 5 minutes, 21 seconds

Smooth Soup

First the program cooks the ingredients in the pitcher, then a unique set of pulsing and blending patterns purées the ingredients into a creamy, luxurious bowl of smooth soup. To get started, check out the chart "How to Make the Perfect Smooth Soup" on page 24. You can also try a comforting bowl of one of my recipes, like Butternut Squash Soup with Pomegranate Seeds (page 77), Black Bean Soup (page 75) or Bacon-Cauliflower Soup (page 96). When the program is complete, you'll want to adjust the soup's consistency as desired with additional broth, and season with salt and pepper. Run time: 30 minutes

Hearty Soup

Unlike other blenders that can only produce one texture, with the Foodi™ Blender, you can not only make a creamy smooth soup, but also a hearty textured soup. Toss in veggies, protein, noodles, and beans for a hearty lunch or dinner. You will love my Rosemary and Lemon White Bean Minestrone Soup (page 85) and my Cajun Corn Chowder (page 89). Don't have the ingredients for either of these recipes? Use the "How to Make the Perfect Hearty Soup" chart on page 25 to freestyle your own soup! Run time: 30 minutes

Sauce/Dip

Cook and blend a variety of ingredients to create creamy sauces, dips, purées, and fondues. With this program you can make both sweet and savory hot dips and sauces like Blackberry and Blueberry Jam Parfait (page 53), Beer and Cheese Dip (page 69), and Marinara Sauce (page 115). Plus the nonstick surface makes easy cleanup for chocolate and cheese sauces like Chocolate Fondue (page 181) or Creamy Garlic Alfredo Sauce (page 118). Run time: 30 minutes, 30 seconds

Mixers

Use this program with sweet and savory ingredients to create bold-flavored simple syrups and concentrates that can be added to your favorite craft cocktails or poured over fizzy water to make homemade sodas. Try Strawberry-Lime Mixer (page 134), Lemon-Ginger

Simple Syrup (page 123), or follow the "How to Make the Perfect Concentrated Mixer" chart on page 27 to make your own flavor combination! Run time: 10 minutes, 30 seconds

Waters

Rapidly infuse water with fruits, herbs, teas, and spices to create comforting warm tonics and refreshing flavored spa waters. Try Lemonade Peach Tea (page 125) or Raspberry-Lime Infused Water (page 127). Run time: 10 minutes, 30 seconds

Cocktails

This program leverages the precision heating element to rapidly infuse spirits and cocktails with bold flavors. Traditionally, this is done by submerging ingredients in the cocktail or spirit for days or weeks. However, this program is designed to heat ingredients to a temperature that promotes the transfer of flavors without burning off any of the alcohol, so you can infuse faster. Now you can make infused spirits like Pineapple-Infused Tequila (page 154) and Habanero-Infused Vodka (page 161), or make infused craft cocktails like my Summertime Sangria (page 167). Run time: 10 minutes, 30 seconds

Manual Functions

With the Foodi™ Blender, you aren't locked into using preset programs. If you can't find an Auto iQ program to fit your needs or if you'd rather freestyle it, try using any of the following manual functions.

Pulse

Use the PULSE button to quickly mix up ingredients. With this button, short bursts of power stir ingredients and promote even cooking.

Blend

In manual mode, you can select from three different blending speeds—low, medium, and high—to get the consistency you desire. BLEND settings will run for 1 minute, unless manually stopped.

Cook

Cook all of your favorite recipes using the manual COOK mode on the Foodi™ Blender. The precision heating element adapts to three different temperatures—low, medium, and high—for perfect results every time. The COOK settings will run for 1 hour, unless manually stopped.

Keep Warm

KEEP WARM turns on automatically once a heated program is complete to keep contents warm for up to 1 hour. This means that your soups and sauces won't get cold if you aren't ready to eat right away.

Clean

The dedicated CLEAN program delivers hassle-free cleaning at the touch of a button. Combining heat with rapid pulses, the seven-minute program easily removes stuck-on ingredients from the

A Few Words About Cleanup

To keep your Foodi Blender in tip-top shape, clean the pitcher and accessories with soap and water after each use. Keep the following in mind:

- When using the CLEAN program, make sure you rinse the pitcher first.
- If you choose to wash the accessories by hand, use the provided cleaning brush to avoid direct contact with the blades. Remember, the pitcher is nonstick to aid in easy cleaning, so refrain from using abrasive cleaning tools.
- While the pitcher, lid, center cap, and tamper are dishwasher safe, do not submerge the glass pitcher in water, as it will damage the integrated heating element.
- To clean the motor base and control panel, wipe with a clean, damp cloth.

base and sides of the pitcher. For best results, give the pitcher a quick rinse, add water and a drop of soap, then secure the lid and press CLEAN. Always rinse and dry the glass pitcher before you use it again to cook. Run time: 6 minutes, 36 seconds

FREQUENTLY ASKED QUESTIONS

Q: How long should I preheat the Foodi™ Blender?
A: When using the Foodi Blender, there is no need to preheat before adding ingredients. Each of the programs and functions incorporate preheating time for the precision heating element to get up to the right temperature. If you want to cook aromatics like onions and garlic before making soups and sauces, use the SAUTÉ program as a first step.

Q: How do I know when my Auto iQ Program is complete?
A: The Foodi Blender is equipped with a countdown timer, so you know exactly how long is left in each Auto iQ Program. When the program is complete, the countdown will read zero and the unit will beep to signify completion.

Q: Why does the blender beep while cooking?
A: When designing the Auto iQ programs, we incorporated a "stir alert" to let you know the unit is about to stir. The alert is 3 beeps followed by a 2 second pause before each stir. When adding ingredients through the center feed hole, do so carefully when the machine beeps.

Q: How do I convert my favorite recipes to the Foodi Blender?
A: You can easily convert your favorite family recipes to the Foodi Blender. Follow my recommendations and charts on pages 23 through 27 for creating your own recipes from scratch.

Q: **If I don't have all of the ingredients for a recipe, can I swap the ingredient with something I do have?**

A: Throughout the recipes in the book, you will find my recommendations for ingredient swaps and suggestions. If the recipe you are making doesn't have a recipe swap noted, confirm the swap you want to make will cook in the same amount of time as the original ingredient. Some swaps are easier to make than others, while some ingredient changes may require adjusting cook times and temperatures. You can also follow the charts on pages 23 through 27 to go freestyle; my advice is to experiment and have fun!

Lavender-Rosemary
Infused Vodka, *page 155*

2

Get Blending! (And Cooking and Infusing . . .)

THE FOODI™ BLENDER IS SO MUCH MORE THAN JUST A blender. Yes, it is great for making quick breakfast smoothies and whole-food juices, like the Carrot Cake Smoothie (page 39) or Beet and Berry Blast (page 38), but you can also make a breakfast you would never expect in a blender, like Banana-Nut Oatmeal (page 49), Blackberry and Blueberry Jam Parfait (page 53), or Simple Hollandaise Sauce (page 33)!

Whether you are making dinner for the family or entertaining a crowd, the Foodi Blender makes mealtime a breeze. In minutes, you can throw together a hearty soup, like my Broccoli-Cheddar Soup (page 91), or blend up Puttanesca Sauce (page 117) to serve over your favorite pasta. Quickly prep for your next party by making Caramelized Onion Dip (page 67) or Roasted Red Pepper Hummus (page 61).

From frozen cocktails, like a Frozen Coconut Mojito (page 147) or Frozen Negroni (page 146), to infused craft cocktails made with Cucumber and Lime Infused Gin (page 156) or Vanilla Bean and

Orange Infused Bourbon (page 157), the Ninja® Foodi™ Blender was designed to make your time in the kitchen more fun—and rewarding.

EQUIPPING YOUR KITCHEN

Here, we'll review the pantry and refrigerator staples that will help you get the most out of your Foodi Blender, as well as some tools that may come in handy.

Super-Simple Staples

Here is a list of the ingredients I always have in my refrigerator and pantry so that I can make a quick and easy breakfast smoothie, blend up soups and sauces, or create craft cocktails and mocktails on the fly.

Broth/Stock: Broths and stocks make a great base for soups and sauces. If the recipe calls for water, you can swap it for vegetable, chicken, or beef broth to add extra flavor.

Canned Tomatoes: Whole, diced, or puréed, tomatoes add acidity, sweetness, and color to a vast array of dishes. It is impractical to assume you will always have fresh tomatoes available, but canned tomatoes provide consistent flavor, even when fresh tomatoes are out of season. Use canned tomatoes for sauces and soups.

Dry Pasta: Whether you prefer penne, rigatoni, or linguine, having dry pasta in the kitchen means you are always prepared for an impromptu meal. Dry pasta is versatile and can be paired with a variety of sauces made in the Foodi Blender. You can also use pasta or egg noodles to make hearty soups.

Extra-Virgin Olive Oil: I keep a variety of oils in the pantry, but EVOO is the hero of most meals. A good olive oil can be used for everything from sautéing to finishing, and everything else in between.

Fresh Fruits: There is a variety of fresh fruit on my shopping list each week, regardless of what recipes I have planned. Apples and bananas add a little sweetness to recipes, and they are also yummy snacks.

Fresh Vegetables: Sweet potatoes, shallots, and squash are a few favorites I keep stocked in the pantry, but this will vary seasonally, depending on what's available.

Frozen Fruit and Berries: I buy frozen fruit and berries such as mangos, pineapple, strawberries, blueberries, and raspberries in bulk so I have them year-round to add to my smoothies. I also freeze bananas, so I always have them on hand.

Garlic: There are three staples that I use in almost every savory recipe throughout this book: olive oil, sea salt, and freshly ground pepper. If I had to choose a fourth, it would be garlic. When sautéed, it adds an amazing depth of flavor.

Granulated Sugar: Granulated sugar can be used with herbs, spices, or fresh fruit to create simple syrups and concentrates for craft cocktails.

Honey: A natural sweetener, honey can be used to add sweetness to smoothies, frozen treats, and desserts.

Lemons and Limes: There aren't many fresh foods on my list of pantry staples, but having lemons and limes available for fresh juice is a must.

Lentils and Beans: Lentils and beans add extra protein, fiber, and a bit of bulk to any soup recipe. Purée for a smooth, creamy soup or add them whole to hearty soups.

Milks: I always have a variety of milks in the refrigerator, from whole milk to almond milk and some cans of coconut milk. Milk is a great thickener in creamy soups and smoothies.

Nuts and Seeds: Not only do nuts and seeds taste great, they add a fabulous crunchy texture to any dish. Store nuts and seeds in a cool, dark place in your pantry to preserve their nutrients and keep them fresh. I recommend keeping almonds, cashews, hazelnuts, pecans, pistachios, pumpkin seeds, sesame seeds, sunflower seeds, and walnuts on hand. Add them on top of soups or blend them into your favorite smoothies for a protein boost.

Onions: Almost every great meal begins with sautéing an onion. Don't worry about keeping all varieties on the counter—a few yellow onions are versatile enough to work in most recipes.

Parmesan Cheese: A small amount packs a lot of flavor! Don't waste your time with grated cheese. Instead, buy a wedge; it will last a while in the refrigerator.

Super-Simple Spice Rack

Long gone are the days when your spices collected cobwebs in the back of your cabinet. With a few simple spices you can pack dense flavor into a variety of soups and sauces. If you don't already have these spices, you don't need to buy them all at once. Plan to pick up a few each time you go to the market.

Basil: Dried basil is delicious in sauces, soups and a variety of marinades.

Black Pepper: My recipes always specify freshly ground black pepper, because freshly ground peppercorns give you the fullest flavor. I have a grinder that is always next to the stove and is constantly being refilled.

Cayenne Pepper: Cayenne is ground from one of the hottest varieties of dried hot peppers and is often optional in recipes. Use it sparingly to add a little kick to your dish.

Cinnamon Sticks: Known for its warm, sweet flavor, cinnamon can be added to both sweet and savory dishes.

Cumin Seeds: Cumin is a popular aromatic spice used in Middle Eastern, Asian, Mediterranean, and Mexican cuisines.

Coriander Seeds: Coriander has a sweet, aromatic taste with a touch of citrus. Grind the seeds into sauces or infuse the flavor into craft cocktails.

Ground Ginger: Aromatic, pungent, and spicy, ginger adds a special flavor and zest to smoothies and infused waters alike.

Oregano: Oregano is classified as either Mediterranean or Mexican and is often used to season dishes from these two regions.

Paprika: Paprika is ground from dried red bell peppers. There are different types of paprika, including smoked and sweet.

Rosemary: Use this delightfully aromatic dried herb in sauces and marinades. Or infuse mixers and cocktails.

Sea Salt: Salt will add flavor to any recipe. It is used in both the sweet and savory recipes throughout this book. Remember: Table salt cannot and should not be substituted 1:1 for sea salt, as it is much finer and will result in an oversalted dish.

Thyme: One of the many herbs used in Italian kitchens, thyme is a primary herb in soups and stews.

Super-Simple Tools and Accessories

There are a few simple accessories that I recommend having on hand when prepping and serving the recipes throughout this book.

Ice Cube Tray

Plastic and silicone ice cube trays are inexpensive and can be used for much more than just making ice. Stock up on a few ice cube trays so you can freeze ingredients for frozen treats, like milk, coffee, wine, and chocolate, etc. You can also use ice cube trays to freeze and store marinades and sauces for future use. Last but not least, an ice cube tray makes for a simple small ice pop mold.

Mason Jars

We use mason jars in place of glasses in our kitchen, but they also make for a convenient to-go cup. Simply fill up the jar with your favorite smoothie and screw on the lid. When you are entertaining, use the mason jars as a fun way to serve up craft cocktails and homemade sodas. It is also a good idea to keep a few smaller mason jars on hand for storing sauces and dressings that you make in your Foodi™ Blender.

Muffin Tin

With the Ninja® Foodi, you can whip up muffin and cupcake batter. Having a muffin tin in your cupboard will come in handy, not only to bake the batters, but also to bake mini frittatas and egg cups.

Plastic Pitcher

Making batch cocktails and mocktails is easy in the Foodi Blender. After rapidly infusing your craft drinks, pour the drink into a plastic pitcher and place the pitcher in the refrigerator to cool.

Ice Pop Molds

Have a specialty ice pop mold you got from the store? Great! You are ready to make Mango Yogurt Ice Pops (page 191). No mold, no problem. Ice cube trays, small disposable cups, and muffin tins lined with foil cupcake wrappers can be used in lieu of an ice pop mold. Blend together your favorite fruits with a little fruit juice, yogurt, or milk and you are good to go!

Accessories to Get More Out of Your Foodi Blender

In addition to the accessories that came with your Foodi Blender, here are a few additional accessories you can purchase to truly get the most out of your blender. All of these accessories are available at NinjaKitchen.com.

Craft Drink Strainer

With professional-grade fine mesh and a conical design, the Craft Drink Strainer allows you to easily strain ingredients after blending them so you can create delicious craft drinks. Use the Craft Drink Strainer to strain aromatics after infusing spirits or to strain fruit from your mulled wine and ciders.

Ninja Over-Ice™ Carafe

The Ninja Over-Ice™ Carafe was designed especially for iced coffee, iced tea, and other cold craft drinks. It has outstanding thermal properties to keep your drinks icy—not to mention, it is durable and condensation-free.

THE MAGIC OF BLENDED RECIPES

Blending is not a new technology; in fact, it is a tried-and-true way to prep ingredients in home kitchens, as well as restaurant kitchens. Our goal when designing the Foodi™ Blender was to take everything you know and love about blending and make it better—and we did just that. The Foodi Blender is so much more than just a smoothie maker. In fact, using it may even make you a better cook.

Elevate Your Cooking

The difference between a home-cooked meal and a restaurant meal is often the sauce that tops off a dish. I'm talking about the puréed veggies nestled under your chicken thigh, a bright vinaigrette atop your greens, or the creamy gravy served over your steak. With the Foodi Blender, you can now create simple, flavor-packed sauces, dressings, and marinades to elevate any dish.

Hands-Off Cooking

Not only will the Foodi Blender elevate the way you cook, but it requires little effort. Long gone are the days standing over the stove stirring your sauces and blending your purées. With this appliance, you merely pile the ingredients into the glass pitcher, select the Auto iQ program, and let the blender get to work.

Easy Cleanup

With the Foodi Blender, you greatly streamline the process of creating a meal, which means that you also minimize your cleanup time. Using the appliance's CLEAN setting makes the job even easier!

Healthful Focus on Fruits and Veggies

It is no secret that blended smoothies are a convenient and delicious way to enjoy your daily serving of fruits and veggies. But now you can blend up fresh vegetables and whole foods into flavorful sauces, sippable soups, and so much more.

How to Make the Perfect Smoothie

Not only do smoothies make for a quick and easy breakfast during a busy week, but they are the perfect way to use up all those odds and ends of fruit in my freezer! Although smoothies can be sweet, they are packed with fruits and vegetables and full of vitamins and nutrients. I love whipping some up for breakfast, for an afternoon treat, or for a healthy sweet tooth fix.

Best of all, you can pull them together with just a few ingredients. I typically use whatever I have on hand, but I have included some of my favorite smoothie recipes in Chapter 3: Breakfasts (page 31). There really is no wrong way to make a smoothie, but below I've outlined my go-to formula for perfect ingredient proportions.

PICK FRESH OR FROZEN FRUIT (1 OR 2 CUPS)	CHOOSE A LIQUID (1 CUP)	SNEAK IN LEAFY GREENS (½ CUP)	KEEP IT COLD (1 CUP)	ADD SOME SUPERFOODS (OPTIONAL)	SWEETEN IT UP (OPTIONAL)
Apple	Almond or other nut milk	Chard	Ice	Bee pollen	Agave syrup
Avocado	Apple juice	Kale		Cacao	Cacao powder
Bananas	Coconut milk	Spinach		Chia seeds	Dates
Blackberries	Coconut water			Goji berries	Honey
Blueberries	Orange juice			Maca	Maple syrup
Grapes	Whole milk			Protein Powder	Nut butter
Mango	Yogurt			Spirulina	
Peaches					
Pineapple					
Raspberries					
Strawberries					

How to Make the Perfect
Smooth Soup (in 35 Minutes)

For a silky, satisfying soup right out of your blender pitcher, follow this basic formula. Serves 3 or 4.

FIRST, BUILD FLAVOR

CHOOSE OIL OR BUTTER (2 TABLESPOONS)	ADD ONION (1 SMALL, PEELED, QUARTERED)	CHOOSE SPICES AND AROMATICS (3 TABLESPOONS TOTAL)	SELECT SAUTÉ
Avocado oil Butter Canola oil Coconut oil Olive oil	Onion Shallot	Coriander seeds Cumin seeds Garlic Ginger Pepper Salt Thyme Tomato Paste	The blender will gently pulse 3 times to chop aromatics and pull them toward the heating element, then it will cook for 5 minutes.

THEN, COOK INGREDIENTS

CHOOSE A VEGGIE (4 CUPS TOTAL, CUT INTO 1-INCH PIECES)	CHOOSE A BASE (4 CUPS TOTAL)	SELECT SMOOTH SOUP
Broccoli Butternut squash Carrots Cauliflower Celery Corn Kale Mushrooms Peppers Potatoes Spinach Sweet potatoes Tomatoes	Beef stock/broth Chicken stock/broth Coconut milk Tomato sauce Vegetable stock/broth Water	The blender will preheat until it reaches a boil. It will then pulse and stir to evenly cook ingredients, after which it will purée into a smooth soup. **PRO TIP:** Add a couple splashes of heavy cream at the end of the program for a creamy texture.

How to Make the Perfect
Hearty Soup (in 35 Minutes)

These steps result in a delicious soup that fills you up and comes together in under an hour. Serves 3 or 4.

FIRST, BUILD FLAVOR

CHOOSE OIL OR BUTTER (2 TABLESPOONS)	ADD ONION (1 SMALL, PEELED, QUARTERED)	CHOOSE SPICES AND AROMATICS (3 TABLESPOONS TOTAL)	SELECT SAUTÉ
Avocado oil	Onion	Coriander seeds	The blender will gently pulse 3 times to chop aromatics and pull them toward the heating element, then it will cook for 5 minutes.
Butter	Shallot	Cumin seeds	
Canola oil		Garlic	
Coconut oil		Ginger	
Olive oil		Pepper	
		Salt	
		Thyme	
		Tomato Paste	

THEN, COOK INGREDIENTS

CHOOSE A VEGGIE (2 CUPS TOTAL, CUT INTO 1-INCH PIECES)	CHOOSE A PROTEIN (1 CUP TOTAL, CUT INTO 1-INCH PIECES, OPTIONAL)	CHOOSE A BASE (3 CUPS TOTAL)	ADD PASTA AND/ OR BEANS (1 CUP TOTAL OR ½ CUP EACH, OPTIONAL)	SELECT HEARTY SOUP
Broccoli	Beef sirloin	Beef stock/ broth	Black beans (cooked or canned)	The blender will preheat until it reaches a boil. It will then gently pulse and stir to evenly cook ingredients.
Butternut squash	Chicken breast	Chicken stock/ broth	Chickpeas	
Carrots	Ham	Coconut milk	Ditalini	
Cauliflower	Pork loin	Tomato sauce	Egg noodles	
Celery	Turkey breast	Vegetable stock/broth	Macaroni (use pasta box instructions for cook time)	
Corn		Water		
Kale			White beans (add beans with 6 minutes remaining in program)	
Mushrooms				
Peppers				
Potatoes				
Spinach				
Sweet potatoes				
Tomatoes				

How to Make the Perfect
Custom Cocktail (in 10 Minutes)

Serve sophisticated craft cocktails at home with this foolproof recipe template.

FIRST, BUILD FLAVOR (OPTIONAL)

	CHOOSE A SPICE (2 TABLESPOONS TOTAL)	SELECT SAUTÉ
Start recipes by toasting spices to unlock and enhance natural flavors, then add the remaining ingredients to heat, blend, and strain.	Black pepper Cardamom Cinnamon sticks Clove Coriander Dried chilies Fennel	The blender will heat to its highest temperature and toast for 5 minutes. **PRO TIP:** Use this first step to unlock flavors with heat like never before.

THEN, COOK INGREDIENTS

CHOOSE A FRESH HERB (2 TEASPOONS TOTAL)	CHOOSE A FLAVOR (2 CUPS TOTAL OF FRESH INGREDIENTS)	CHOOSE A LIQUID (4 CUPS TOTAL)	SELECT COCKTAIL
Basil Ginger Loose-leaf tea Mint Rosemary Turmeric Vanilla extract	Apple Blueberries Cherries Lemons (quartered) Orange (quartered) Pineapple Raspberries Strawberries Watermelon	Bourbon Gin Rum Tequila Vodka Whiskey	The blender will heat and automatically stir your ingredients by gently pulsing. **PRO TIP:** Strain ingredients into a heat-proof container. Chill, then serve or mix as desired.

How to Make the Perfect
Concentrated Mixer (in 10 Minutes)

Combine your concentrated mixer with water, seltzer, or your favorite spirit.
Take dessert to the next level by pouring mixers over ice cream or snow cones.

FIRST, BUILD FLAVOR (OPTIONAL)

Start recipes by toasting spices to unlock and enhance natural flavors, then add the remaining ingredients to heat, blend, and strain.

CHOOSE A SPICE (2 TABLESPOONS TOTAL)	SELECT SAUTÉ
Black pepper Cardamom Cinnamon sticks Clove Coriander Dried chilies Fennel	The blender will heat to its highest temperature and toast for 5 minutes. **PRO TIP:** Use this first step to unlock flavors with heat like never before.

THEN, COOK INGREDIENTS

ADD WATER (1 CUP)	CHOOSE A SWEETENER (1 TO 1½ CUPS TOTAL, OPTIONAL)	CHOOSE A FLAVOR (2 CUPS TOTAL OF FRESH INGREDIENTS)	CHOOSE A FRESH HERB (4 CUPS TOTAL)	SELECT MIXER
	Agave nectar Honey Maple syrup Sugar	Blueberries Cherries Lemons Orange Pineapple Raspberries Strawberries Watermelon	Basil Ginger Loose-leaf tea (green/black/red) Mint Rosemary Turmeric Vanilla extract	The blender will heat and automatically stir ingredients by gently pulsing. **PRO TIP:** Strain ingredients into a heat-proof container.

ABOUT THE RECIPES

Before diving in, let's break down how I structured the book and how you should approach the recipes throughout. As you begin, remember to read through each recipe completely and gather all the ingredients you need in advance. As with everything else, a little prep work before you begin to cook will save you time in the long run.

I also suggest that you follow each recipe exactly as written your first time trying it. Then, as you become more comfortable with the Foodi™ Blender, you can switch things up and try swapping ingredients.

Labels

I have included a variety of labels to guide you through the recipes. You will find dietary labels (Dairy-free, Gluten-free, Nut-free, Vegetarian, and Vegan) so you know which recipes fit with your lifestyle and which you can modify slightly to make work for you. All recipes also include nutritional information.

You will also note the following labels so you can find the perfect recipe for every meal:

Under 30 Minutes Perfect for busy weeknights, these recipes are Foodi Blender-to-table in 30 minutes or less.

Family Favorite A selection of the recipes that are on repeat in my house

5-Ingredient Recipes that require just 5 ingredients (or fewer!)

Time

The recipes that fill the following chapters include a breakdown of how long the recipe will take, start to finish. I've included the prep time, and total cook, blend, and cooling times (depending on the recipe), so you can find the recipe that works best for the time you have available.

Tips

To help you make the most of your Foodi™ Blender and the recipes in the following chapters, I have provided my most helpful tips and tricks. You will find the following tips highlighted throughout the recipes:

Substitution Tip Follow my recommendations for swapping ingredients in and out. These are my best ideas for changing up the flavor profile or subbing ingredients for allergy reasons. For example: Don't have honey? Try maple syrup.

Variation Tip This is where we help you customize the recipes to add a personal touch!

Did you Know? Here I showcase specific ingredients, sharing details on selecting or buying them, working with them, and storing them.

Hack It My best cooking shortcuts and tricks that will make prepping the recipe even easier.

Nutritional Stats

Each recipe includes a complete nutritional profile, so you can have a good handle on the breakdown of every recipe—including calories, fat, macronutrients, and some micronutrients.

Finally, above all else, remember to have fun! What are you waiting for? It's time to get blending, cooking, and infusing!

Blueberry-Banana
Smoothie, *page 32*

3

Breakfasts

Blueberry-Banana Smoothie

SERVES 2

This creamy and refreshing blueberry smoothie is made with frozen blueberries, banana, plain yogurt, and a splash of milk, all blended together into a frosty drink. This smoothie recipe is not only delicious, but also an easy breakfast or snack. All of the ingredients go into the Foodi™ Blender and, with the push of a button, you have a super smooth and creamy smoothie. That's all there is to it! If you want to add some mix-ins, try flaxseed, chia seeds, or some greens, like spinach.

GLUTEN-FREE, NUT-FREE, VEGETARIAN, UNDER 30 MINUTES, 5-INGREDIENT

PREP TIME: 5 minutes
BLEND TIME: 1 minute

SUBSTITUTION TIP:
I love using frozen fruit in my smoothies, because I always have my freezer stocked. If you don't have frozen fruit, you can swap out fresh for frozen. Just be sure to add about ½ cup of ice to get the icy-cold consistency that you crave!

2 cups frozen blueberries

1 banana, peeled and halved

2 cups plain yogurt

¼ cup milk

1. Place the blueberries, banana, yogurt, and milk into the blender pitcher in the order listed.

2. Select SMOOTHIE.

3. Pour into two glasses and enjoy.

Per serving: Calories: 299; Total fat: 10g; Saturated fat: 6g; Cholesterol: 35mg; Sodium: 127mg; Carbohydrates: 45g; Fiber: 6g; Protein: 11g

Simple Hollandaise Sauce

Hollandaise can be intimidating to make at home, which is why most people only indulge in this decadent treat when they are out to brunch (hello, Eggs Benedict). However, making this butter-based sauce couldn't be easier. Whiz it up and serve it spooned over poached eggs, spread over roasted fish, or drizzled on top of roasted veggies.

GLUTEN-FREE, NUT-FREE, VEGETARIAN, UNDER 30 MINUTES

PREP TIME: 5 minutes
COOK TIME: 5 minutes
BLEND TIME: 30 seconds

VARIATION TIP: Transform this hollandaise into a béarnaise sauce with two simple additions. Add 3 tablespoons minced shallot along with the butter in step 1, then add 1 tablespoon fresh tarragon in step 2 before blending.

8 tablespoons unsalted butter

3 egg yolks

1 tablespoon lemon juice

Pinch sea salt

¼ teaspoon Dijon mustard

Pinch cayenne pepper or hot sauce (optional)

1. Place the butter into the blender pitcher. Select SAUTÉ.

2. Add the egg yolks, lemon juice, salt, Dijon, and cayenne or hot sauce (if using), and select BLEND then LOW and run for about 30 seconds, until the color has lightened and the ingredients are fully incorporated.

Per serving: *Calories: 161; Total fat: 17g; Saturated fat: 10g; Cholesterol: 145mg; Sodium: 38mg; Carbohydrates: 1g; Fiber: 0g; Protein: 2g*

Tropical Greens Smoothie

A version of this smoothie made an appearance in my first cookbook—Paleo in 28. In fact, it was developed in my first Ninja® Blender years ago and has been on rotation in our house ever since. It is a simple, 5-ingredient recipe, and one that is sure to become a favorite in your house as well. The tropical flavors of mango, pineapple, and coconut are refreshing and easily hide the serving of spinach that I sneak in. Green, yet perfectly fruity and sweet, this is the ideal beginner green smoothie for adults and kids alike.

DAIRY-FREE, GLUTEN-FREE, NUT-FREE, VEGAN, UNDER 30 MINUTES, FAMILY FAVORITE, 5-INGREDIENT

PREP TIME: 5 minutes
BLEND TIME: 2 minutes

VARIATION TIP: For a richer, creamier smoothie, replace the coconut water in this recipe with coconut milk. I like to use the full-fat version from the can.

---

1 cup frozen mango chunks

1 cup frozen pineapple chunks

2 cups baby spinach

1 cup coconut water

2 bananas, peeled and halved

1. Place the mango, pineapple, spinach, coconut water, and banana into the blender pitcher in the order listed.

2. Select EXTRACT.

3. Pour into two glasses and enjoy.

Per serving: Calories: 210; Total fat: 1g; Saturated fat: 0g; Cholesterol: 0mg; Sodium: 153mg; Carbohydrates: 52g; Fiber: 6g; Protein: 4g

Creamy Avocado Smoothie

SERVES 2

Smoothies are definitely not boring; in fact, there are thousands of possible combinations of fruits, vegetables, milks, and juices to brighten up your morning. I enjoy trying new combinations and getting creative, but there was one ingredient I was always hesitant to add to smoothies—avocados. You may also be thinking, "Avocado in a smoothie?" Turns out there is a reason that you find avocados in everything these days, from savory to sweet recipes. They are versatile and delicious! Avocado adds a velvety creaminess to this tasty smoothie.

DAIRY-FREE, GLUTEN-FREE, NUT-FREE, VEGAN, UNDER 30 MINUTES

PREP TIME: 5 minutes
BLEND TIME: 2 minutes

VARIATION TIP: Put your own twist on this recipe by swapping out the pineapple with your favorite frozen fruit, add spice with a bit of ginger, or add protein with hempseed.

1 cup ice

½ cup frozen pineapple chunks

1 frozen banana, peeled and quartered

½ avocado, peeled and pitted

2 cups baby spinach

1 cup full-fat coconut milk

1. Place the ice, pineapple, banana, avocado, spinach, and coconut milk into the blender pitcher in the order listed.

2. Select EXTRACT.

3. Pour into two glasses and enjoy.

Per serving: Calories: 350; Total fat: 30g; Saturated fat: 22g; Cholesterol: 0mg; Sodium: 42mg; Carbohydrates: 24g; Fiber: 4g; Protein: 5g

Beet and Berry Blast

SERVES 2

If you're looking to sneak more fruits and veggies into your diet, smoothies are a great place to start. If you aren't ready to dive headfirst into green smoothies packed with kale and spinach or are looking for something just a bit sweeter, this Beet and Berry Blast is a great place to start. The sweetness of the strawberries, raspberries, and banana mask the earthiness of the beet. And the vibrant magenta hue is quite swoon-worthy!

In most smoothie recipes that use beet as an ingredient, you need to cook or grate the beet. However the Foodi™ Blender is powerful enough to pulverize tough ingredients, making easy work of a tough, raw beet.

DAIRY-FREE, GLUTEN-FREE, VEGAN, UNDER 30 MINUTES

PREP TIME: 5 minutes
BLEND TIME: 2 minutes

DID YOU KNOW? Packed with essential vitamins and minerals, beets also have a slight sweetness, making them a great (bright pink!) option to sneak nutrients into your kids' morning smoothies.

1 cup frozen strawberries

1 cup frozen raspberries

½ beet, washed, peeled, and sliced

1 banana, peeled and halved

1 cup almond milk

1 tablespoon maple syrup

1. Place the strawberries, raspberries, beet slices, banana, almond milk, and maple syrup into the blender pitcher in the order listed.

2. Select SMOOTHIE.

3. Pour into two glasses and enjoy.

Per serving: Calories: 277; Total fat: 2g; Saturated fat: 0g; Cholesterol: 0mg; Sodium: 97mg; Carbohydrates: 67g; Fiber: 10g; Protein: 3g

Carrot Cake Smoothie

SERVES 2

Smoothies are not just a convenient way to eat more fruits and vegetables, but I have found that they are also a fun way to enjoy the flavors of your favorite desserts in a healthier way. In this recipe, I brought together all of the classic flavors of a classic carrot cake in a rich and creamy smoothie. Not only does this recipe sneak in fresh carrots, but you also get creamy protein-rich almond butter, warm cinnamon, and spicy ginger. Enjoy for breakfast—or dessert!

GLUTEN-FREE, VEGETARIAN, UNDER 30 MINUTES

PREP TIME: 5 minutes
BLEND TIME: 2 minutes

VARIATION TIP: Turn this smoothie into a smoothie bowl by omitting ½ cup almond milk from the recipe. This will ensure the base is thicker and can support the smoothie bowl toppings, like sliced banana, coconut flakes, toasted walnuts, and a drizzle of almond butter.

2 frozen bananas, peeled and quartered

2 carrots, washed, peeled, and cut into 1½-inch pieces

1 cup almond milk

½ cup vanilla Greek yogurt

1 tablespoon almond butter

¼ teaspoon ground cinnamon

1 (1-inch) piece ginger, peeled and quartered

1. Place the bananas, carrots, almond milk, yogurt, almond butter, cinnamon, and ginger into the blender pitcher in the order listed.

2. Select EXTRACT.

3. Pour into two glasses and enjoy.

Per serving: Calories: 233; Total fat: 8g; Saturated fat: 2g; Cholesterol: 8mg; Sodium: 147mg; Carbohydrates: 37g; Fiber: 5g; Protein: 6g

Summer Strawberry Smoothie

SERVES 2

Warm weather, sunny skies, and spending time with friends are a few reasons I love summer months, but perhaps my favorite thing about summer is that it is the peak season for so many fruits and berries. Growing up, I loved going berry picking, snacking on juicy strawberries as we filled our baskets. I remember coming home covered in the sticky sweet juice, smiling from ear to ear. In this Summer Strawberry Smoothie, I brought together all of my favorite summer flavors for a bright, refreshing breakfast (or afternoon) treat.

DAIRY-FREE, GLUTEN-FREE, NUT-FREE, VEGETARIAN, VEGAN, UNDER 30 MINUTES, FAMILY FAVORITE, 5-INGREDIENT

PREP TIME: 5 minutes
BLEND TIME: 1 minute

VARIATION TIP: This recipe was developed for when fresh strawberries are at their peak, but if you don't have fresh strawberries, don't fret! You can swap fresh for frozen and it will be equally delicious! If you want an extra creamy smoothie, add a banana or ½ cup plain Greek yogurt.

1 cup frozen mango chunks
2 cups fresh strawberries
1 cup orange juice
Juice of 1 lemon

1. Place the mango, strawberries, orange juice, and lemon juice into the blender pitcher in the order listed.
2. Select SMOOTHIE.
3. Pour into two glasses, and enjoy.

Per serving: *Calories: 167; Total fat: 1g; Saturated fat: 0g; Cholesterol: 0mg; Sodium: 6mg; Carbohydrates: 43g; Fiber: 5g; Protein: 2g*

Mango-Berry Protein Smoothie

SERVES 2

If you are strapped for time in the morning and are looking for a healthy, easy fix, try this Mango-Berry Protein Smoothie. It also works as a filling meal replacement because it is packed with protein. Trust me, it'll be much easier to roll out of bed in the morning when you have this sweet treat to look forward to.

GLUTEN-FREE, NUT-FREE, VEGETARIAN, UNDER 30 MINUTES

PREP TIME: 5 minutes
BLEND TIME: 1 minute

DID YOU KNOW? There are so many easy ways to add protein to your morning smoothie! This version uses protein powder, but you can also add Greek yogurt, nut butter, avocado, hempseed, chia seeds, or oats to ramp up the protein content.

1 banana, peeled and quartered

½ cup ice

½ cup frozen mango chunks

½ cup frozen mixed berries

1 cup milk

¼ cup vanilla protein powder

1. Place the banana, ice, mango, berries, milk, and protein powder into the blender pitcher in the order listed.

2. Select SMOOTHIE.

3. Pour into two glasses and enjoy.

Per serving: *Calories: 277; Total fat: 6g; Saturated fat: 2g; Cholesterol: 12mg; Sodium: 62mg; Carbohydrates: 32g; Fiber: 3g; Protein: 29g*

Peanut Butter and Jelly Smoothie

SERVES 2

Is there a more classic combination than peanut butter and jelly? Whether you are enjoying the traditional lunchbox favorite between two pieces of bread, on a toasted bagel, or in this smoothie, the combination of creamy peanut butter and sweet jelly is as delicious as it is nostalgic. Cooking the berries in the Foodi™ Blender before blending sets this recipe apart. The berries get sticky sweet, just like your favorite childhood jelly.

GLUTEN-FREE, VEGETARIAN, UNDER 30 MINUTES, FAMILY FAVORITE, 5-INGREDIENT

PREP TIME: 5 minutes
COOK TIME: 5 minutes
BLEND TIME: 2 minutes

SUBSTITUTION TIP: Easily customize smoothies to fit your dietary preferences. If you are dairy-free, simply swap milk and yogurt for a dairy-free version, like almond milk or coconut milk yogurt. Allergic to peanuts? Swap peanut butter for almond or cashew butter.

1 cup fresh blueberries
1 cup frozen mixed berries
1 frozen banana
1 cup Greek yogurt
2 tablespoons peanut butter

1. Place the fresh blueberries into the blender pitcher.

2. Select SAUTÉ.

3. Add the mixed berries, banana, yogurt, and peanut butter, then select SMOOTHIE.

4. Pour into two glasses and enjoy.

Per serving: *Calories: 298; Total fat: 13g; Saturated fat: 5g; Cholesterol: 16mg; Sodium: 63mg; Carbohydrates: 40g; Fiber: 7g; Protein: 11g*

Vanilla Almond Milk

MAKES 10 SERVINGS

Homemade Vanilla Almond Milk may sound intimidating, but it is actually pretty simple and only takes a few minutes of active prep time. I love to make a batch over the weekend and then I store it in the refrigerator to use for the week. Include a splash in your morning coffee, add a cup to your favorite smoothie, or enjoy it on its own! If you are looking for an unsweetened version, simply omit the maple syrup. You can also swap the maple syrup for honey or pitted dates.

DAIRY-FREE, GLUTEN-FREE, VEGAN, 5-INGREDIENT

PREP TIME: 5 minutes, plus 6 hours to soak almonds
BLEND TIME: 2 minutes
CHILL TIME: 2 hours

DID YOU KNOW? The leftover almond mixture after straining the milk makes a delicious addition to oatmeal, muffins, and smoothies. Simply spread it out on a parchment paper-lined baking sheet and heat on your oven's lowest setting until completely dry. Almond meal keeps in the freezer for several months and tastes great in baked goodies.

2 cups raw almonds, soaked and strained
5 cups water
Pinch sea salt
2 teaspoons vanilla extract
2 teaspoons maple syrup (optional)

1. Place the almonds, water, salt, vanilla extract, and maple syrup (if using) into the blender pitcher in the order listed.

2. Select BLEND then HIGH and run for 1 minute. Then press HIGH again and run for 1 more minute.

3. Set a large strainer over a medium bowl, and place a nut bag or cheesecloth in the strainer. Pour half the blended mixture into the strainer, then squeeze the milk out of the bag or cheesecloth into the bowl. Remove the ground almonds from the bag or cheesecloth, then repeat the process with the remaining mixture.

4. Chill the almond milk for at least 2 hours before serving. The milk keeps in the refrigerator for 3 to 5 days.

Per serving: Calories: 146; Total fat: 13g; Saturated fat: 1g; Cholesterol: 0mg; Sodium: 7mg; Carbohydrates: 5g; Fiber: 3g; Protein: 5g

Blueberry Pie Smoothie Bowl

SERVES 2

All of your favorite flavors of a warm blueberry pie in a cool and refreshing frozen treat. Sweet blueberries are cooked and then blended with warm spices and topped with crunchy granola. Enjoy for breakfast or whip up a batch for dessert. Blueberries not in season? Try raspberries, strawberries, or even apples!

DAIRY-FREE, VEGAN, UNDER 30 MINUTES

PREP TIME: 5 minutes
COOK TIME: 5 minutes
BLEND TIME: 2 minutes

DID YOU KNOW?
Heating fresh blueberries before blending adds a boost of flavor, just like blueberry jam or a blueberry pie filling is sweeter than fresh blueberries. You can use the SAUTÉ function to boost flavors with a variety of ingredients, like berries in a smoothie or onions in a soup.

1 cup fresh blueberries
1 cup frozen blueberries
2 frozen bananas
½ cup oats
¾ cup almond milk
1 tablespoon almond butter
¼ teaspoon ground cinnamon
½ cup vegan granola (optional)
½ cup fresh blueberries (optional)
1 tablespoon almond butter (optional)

1. Place the fresh blueberries in the blender pitcher.

2. Select SAUTÉ.

3. Add the frozen blueberries, bananas, oats, almond milk, almond butter, and cinnamon, then select SMOOTHIE.

4. Pour into two glasses.

5. If using, top each glass with ¼ cup granola, ¼ cup fresh blueberries, and ½ tablespoon almond butter. Enjoy!

Per serving: Calories: 330; Total fat: 8g; Saturated fat: 1g; Cholesterol: 0mg; Sodium: 79mg; Carbohydrates: 62g; Fiber: 9g; Protein: 7g

Banana-Nut Oatmeal

Oatmeal ranks as my personal favorite in winter months, when every meal is an excuse to warm up. I used to make the quick packets of oatmeal until I learned that it was just as easy to make oatmeal from scratch. Plus, you can easily recreate all of your favorite flavors. This version of Banana-Nut Oatmeal is packed with warm spices, sweet bananas, and crunchy walnuts.

DAIRY-FREE, VEGAN, UNDER 30 MINUTES

PREP TIME: 5 minutes
COOK TIME: 5 minutes

SUBSTITUTION TIP:
If you are nut-free, you can make a few simple swaps to this recipe so that it fits in your diet. Swap almond milk with whole milk, and swap the walnuts with coconut flakes or hempseed.

1 banana, sliced, divided
½ cup rolled oats
½ cup water
⅓ cup almond milk
½ tablespoon maple syrup
1 teaspoon nutmeg
½ teaspoon cinnamon
Pinch sea salt
¼ cup walnuts

1. Place half of the banana, the oats, water, almond milk, maple syrup, nutmeg, cinnamon, and salt into the blender pitcher in the order listed.

2. Select COOK then HIGH and run for 5 minutes.

3. Divide the oatmeal between two bowls and top with the remaining banana and walnuts, as desired.

Per serving: Calories: 316; Total fat: 12g; Saturated fat: 1g; Cholesterol: 0mg; Sodium: 27mg; Carbohydrates: 45g; Fiber: 11g; Protein: 10g

Dutch Baby Pancake with Strawberry Compote

SERVES 4

One of my fondest memories will always be breakfast at my grandma's house. Whenever my cousins and I would pop by, she'd serve up freshly made pancakes and Belgian waffles. Whether we were spending the weekend while our parents were out of town, stopping by before the big high school football game, or visiting while back home from college, we all congregated around Grandma's table. This recipe for a Dutch Baby Pancake with Strawberry Compote encourages you to be the host(ess) with the most(est), just like Grandma. With the Foodi™ Blender, you can easily whip up brunch for a crowd or a decadent breakfast for two!

NUT-FREE, VEGETARIAN, FAMILY FAVORITE

PREP TIME: 15 minutes
BLEND TIME: 10 to 30 seconds
COOK TIME: 30 minutes

HACK IT: From crepes and pancakes to waffles and muffins, the Foodi Blender makes quick work of all types of breakfast and dessert batters. When you're done, use the CLEAN feature, and cleanup is a breeze.

For the Dutch baby

3 tablespoons unsalted butter

3 large eggs

¾ cup all-purpose flour

¾ cup milk

1 tablespoon sugar

½ teaspoon vanilla extract

Pinch sea salt

For the strawberry compote

3 cups fresh strawberries, ends trimmed

1 cup granulated sugar

1 tablespoon lemon juice

2 teaspoons fruit pectin

To make the Dutch baby

1. Preheat the oven to 425ºF.

2. In a 10-inch cast iron skillet, add the butter and place in the oven until the butter is melted and bubbly, not burned, about 3 minutes.

3. Place the eggs into the blender pitcher. Select BLEND then HIGH and run for about 20 seconds, until pale, fluffy, and bubbly.

4. Add the flour, milk, sugar, vanilla, and salt into the blender pitcher and select PULSE until just combined.

5. Pour the batter into the prepared skillet. Return the skillet to the oven and bake for about 15 minutes.

6. Turn the oven off and leave the skillet in the oven for 5 minutes more. Remove the Dutch baby from oven.

To make the strawberry compote

1. Rinse the blender pitcher and place the strawberries, sugar, lemon juice, and fruit pectin into the pitcher in the order listed. PULSE 3 times, then select SAUCE/DIP.

2. Dollop the compote on top of the Dutch baby as desired.

3. Pour the leftover compote into a heat-safe glass container and store in the refrigerator for up to 1 week.

Per serving: *Calories: 495; Total fat: 14g; Saturated fat: 7g; Cholesterol: 186mg; Sodium: 140mg; Carbohydrates: 85g; Fiber: 3g; Protein: 10g*

Blackberry and Blueberry Jam Parfait

SERVES 6 TO 8

This recipe was developed in honor of my husband, who always orders a parfait at our local bakery despite the endless options of delectably sweet breakfast pastries. While a parfait is traditionally made up of yogurt, granola, and fruit, the layer of homemade jam in this parfait is what makes it special. I love the combination of sweet blueberries and blackberries that perfectly complements the tartness of the Greek yogurt. Top with granola, nuts, and seeds if you desire, or enjoy as-is.

GLUTEN-FREE, NUT-FREE, UNDER 30 MINUTES, 5-INGREDIENT

PREP TIME: 10 minutes
COOK TIME: 30 minutes
CHILL TIME: 2 hours

VARIATION TIP: Using the method outlined above, you can create a variety of jams and jellies using your favorite fruits. Try strawberries, raspberries, mixed berries, apricots, and more! You can use fresh or thawed, frozen fruits.

1½ **cups fresh blueberries**
1½ **cups fresh blackberries**
1 **cup granulated sugar**
1 **tablespoon lemon juice**
2 **teaspoons fruit pectin**
Greek yogurt, for serving
Granola, for serving (optional)

1. Place the blueberries, blackberries, sugar, lemon juice, and fruit pectin into the blender pitcher in the order listed.

2. PULSE 3 times, then select SAUCE/DIP.

3. Transfer the jam into a heat-safe glass container and chill at least 2 hours in the refrigerator.

4. When ready to serve, layer the berry jam, Greek yogurt, and granola (if using) as desired in small glasses to create a parfait.

Per serving: Calories: 131; Total fat: 0g; Saturated fat: 0g; Cholesterol: 0mg; Sodium: 4mg; Carbohydrates: 34g; Fiber: 2g; Protein: 1g

The Fluffiest Cheesy Scrambled Eggs

SERVES 4

I strongly believe that "putting an egg on it" transforms almost anything into a meal. But why settle for a boring fried egg when you could add fluffy, cheesy scrambled eggs? I know what you're thinking: Do I really need a recipe for scrambled eggs? Well, this recipe is a bit more of a hack for achieving The Fluffiest Cheesy Scrambled Eggs of all time—and it is all possible thanks to the Foodi™ Blender.

GLUTEN-FREE, NUT-FREE, VEGETARIAN, UNDER 30 MINUTES, FAMILY FAVORITE

PREP TIME: 5 minutes
BLEND TIME: 30 seconds
COOK TIME: 3 to 5 minutes

VARIATION TIP: Go gourmet with your scrambled eggs. Omit the cheese and add ½ teaspoon soy sauce to the blender pitcher before blending. Then stir thinly sliced scallions into your eggs halfway through cooking. Voilà!

1 tablespoon unsalted butter

6 eggs

3 tablespoons milk

¼ cup shredded cheddar cheese

¼ teaspoon sea salt

⅛ teaspoon freshly ground black pepper

1. Heat the butter in a nonstick skillet over medium-low heat.

2. Place the eggs, milk, cheddar cheese, salt, and pepper into the blender pitcher in the order listed.

3. Select MEDIUM and blend for about 30 seconds, until the eggs are uniform and frothy.

4. Once the butter has melted, pour the egg mixture into the preheated pan. Stir with a wooden spoon, scraping the bottom as you go, until all the eggs are cooked, and no visible liquid remains.

Per serving: *Calories: 167; Total fat: 13g; Saturated fat: 6g; Cholesterol: 333mg; Sodium: 373mg; Carbohydrates: 1g; Fiber: 0g; Protein: 12g*

Tomatillo Salsa, *page 58*

4

Appetizers and Dips

Tomatillo Salsa

Blenders have long been used to make quick work of dips, like traditional tomato-based salsas. Toss in a handful of simple ingredients and with a few pulses you have a fresh, vibrant salsa. What sets the Foodi™ Blender apart in this recipe is the ability to sauté the tomatillos before blending the salsa. Raw tomatillos are very acidic and cooking them reduces the acidity and gives them a nice smokiness. Usually this step would be done on the stovetop, but with the Foodi, it is all done in one pitcher!

DAIRY-FREE, GLUTEN-FREE, NUT-FREE, VEGAN, UNDER 30 MINUTES

PREP TIME: 5 minutes
COOK TIME: 5 minutes
BLEND TIME: 1 minute

HACK IT: Looking to spice things up even more? Leave the membrane and seeds in the jalapeños before you blend them. The heat in a hot pepper actually lies in the membrane that connects the seeds to the rest of the pepper, not in the seeds.

1 teaspoon vegetable oil

1½ pounds tomatillos, husked, rinsed, and chopped

½ white onion, coarsely chopped

3 cloves garlic

½ cup cilantro leaves

1 tablespoon lime juice

2 jalapeño peppers, stemmed and cored (remove the seeds and membrane)

Sea salt, to taste

1. Place the vegetable oil and chopped tomatillos into the blender pitcher. Select SAUTÉ.

2. Remove the pitcher lid and let the contents cool for about 5 minutes.

3. Add the onion, garlic, cilantro, lime juice, jalapeño, and salt into the blender pitcher. PULSE 3 times, select BLEND, then choose HIGH and run for about 20 seconds. Repeat until the desired consistency is reached.

4. Stored in an airtight container, this keeps in the refrigerator for up to 1 week.

Per serving: *Calories: 51; Total fat: 2g; Saturated fat: 1g; Cholesterol: 0mg; Sodium: 3mg; Carbohydrates: 9g; Fiber: 3g; Protein: 1g*

Simple Swiss Cheese Fondue

SERVES 8

A little bit retro and a lot bit gooey, this Simple Swiss Cheese Fondue has just 5 simple ingredients. Toss the ingredients in the Foodi™ Blender and voilà, you will return to a pitcher of piping-hot cheesy goodness. To serve, pour the fondue in a serving bowl alongside a variety of things to dunk and some toothpicks for easy dipping. I like to serve this fondue with bread cubes and veggies, but you can also serve it with fruits, like apples and pears. In addition to being a great dip, you can use this recipe as a cheesy topping for your favorite roasted veggies.

GLUTEN-FREE, NUT-FREE, VEGETARIAN, FAMILY FAVORITE, 5-INGREDIENT

PREP TIME: 5 minutes
COOK TIME: 30 minutes

VARIATION TIP: If you want to switch up the cheese used in your fondue, I recommend trying a combination of Gruyère, fontina, and Gouda cheese, about ½ cup of each.

¾ **cup dry white wine**
1 **clove garlic**
1 **teaspoon lemon juice**

2 **(8-ounce) packages sliced Swiss cheese, torn in halves**
1 **tablespoon cornstarch**

1. Place wine, garlic, lemon juice, Swiss cheese, and cornstarch into the blender pitcher in the order listed.

2. Select SAUCE/DIP.

3. Enjoy while warm.

Per serving: *Calories: 236; Total fat: 16g; Saturated fat: 10g; Cholesterol: 52mg; Sodium: 109mg; Carbohydrates: 5g; Fiber: 0g; Protein: 15g*

Roasted Red Pepper Hummus

SERVES 4

Hummus is a staple in our house, and we are firm believers that homemade hummus tastes the best. That's not to say we've never purchased a tub for convenience when entertaining or traveling, but there is no comparison to the flavor you are able to build with this homemade version. This features roasted red peppers, but you can easily switch up the flavor based on your preference (think: roasted garlic, fresh herbs, or briny olives). For a more traditional version, omit the red peppers and basil.

DAIRY-FREE, GLUTEN-FREE, VEGAN, UNDER 30 MINUTES

PREP TIME: 5 minutes
BLEND TIME: 45 seconds

HACK IT: Prepping for a party? Make this up to 3 days in advance and store in an airtight container in the refrigerator.

1 (15-ounce) can chickpeas, drained

1 cup roasted red peppers, drained

8 basil leaves

4 cloves garlic

¼ cup tahini

2 tablespoons extra-virgin olive oil

Juice of 1 lemon

1. Place the chickpeas, roasted red peppers, basil, garlic, tahini, olive oil, and lemon juice into the blender pitcher in the order listed.

2. Select BLEND, then choose HIGH. Blend for 45 seconds or until the desired consistency is reached.

Per serving: Calories: 266; Total fat: 15g; Saturated fat: 2g; Cholesterol: 0mg; Sodium: 281mg; Carbohydrates: 28g; Fiber: 6g; Protein: 8g

Veggies and Lemon-Garlic Whipped Feta Dip

SERVES 6

Do you remember that episode of Friends *when Monica is disappointed that everyone is hanging out at the guys' apartment? She says, "I'm always the hostess!... Even when I was little ... the girls brought their dollies to my tea party." Well, let's just say I related to Monica in that moment. I love entertaining and feeding my friends and family. So, when you come to our house, you know I will put out a spread. A platter of Veggies and Lemon-Garlic Whipped Feta Dip is a staple when we entertain. Whether we are hosting game night or a family holiday, this recipe is easy to whip up at a moment's notice but still tastes fresh and delicious.*

GLUTEN-FREE, NUT-FREE, VEGETARIAN, UNDER 30 MINUTES

PREP TIME: 5 minutes
BLEND TIME: 1 minute

VARIATION TIP: For even more flavor, drizzle 1 tablespoon of Basil Pesto (page 113) on top of the dip just before serving.

1 pound feta cheese, coarsely crumbled

½ cup plain Greek yogurt

1 garlic clove

Zest of 1 lemon

Freshly ground black pepper, to taste

Vegetable crudités, for serving

1. Place the feta cheese, Greek yogurt, garlic, lemon zest, and black pepper into the blender pitcher in the order listed.

2. Select BLEND, then choose LOW. Blend for 1 minute or until the desired consistency is reached.

3. Serve alongside a plate of cut fresh veggies: carrots, celery, and peppers.

4. Stored in an airtight container, this keeps in the refrigerator for 3 or 4 days.

Per serving: Calories: 210; Total fat: 17g; Saturated fat: 12g; Cholesterol: 70mg; Sodium: 843mg; Carbohydrates: 4g; Fiber: 0g; Protein: 11g

Crostini with Ricotta and Jam

SERVES 8

I think one of my favorite functions of the Foodi™ Blender is the ability to make jams, jellies, and compotes from fresh fruit. Not only is fresh jam delicious, but it lets you use up leftover fruit before it goes bad. While I know how to make jams and jellies on the stovetop, I never wanted to spend time watching over the pot, mashing the fruit, and ensuring that it cooks down without burning. With the Foodi Blender, I don't have to babysit the stove. I simply toss in the ingredients, push a button, and walk away. About 30 minutes later, fresh, hot jam is ready to go! Then I use the CLEAN function, so cleanup is a breeze.

The best way to enjoy fresh jam? Paired with crusty bread and fresh ricotta. Perfect for breakfast, an appetizer, or a little after-dinner treat.

NUT-FREE, VEGETARIAN

PREP TIME: 5 minutes
BLEND TIME: 30 minutes

3 cups fresh raspberries

1 cup granulated sugar

1 tablespoon lemon juice

4 teaspoons fruit pectin

**4 bread slices
(I recommend whole-wheat sourdough)**

½ cup fresh ricotta

Pinch sea salt

1. Place the raspberries, sugar, lemon juice, and fruit pectin into the blender pitcher. PULSE 3 times, then select SAUCE/DIP.

2. Meanwhile, in a toaster, toast the bread to your desired doneness and quarter each piece of toast.

3. When the raspberry jam is complete, top the toast with jam, ricotta, and a sprinkle of sea salt.

Per serving: *Calories: 182; Total fat: 2g; Saturated fat: 1g; Cholesterol: 8mg; Sodium: 72mg; Carbohydrates: 39g; Fiber: 3g; Protein: 3g*

White Bean Hummus

SERVES 4

Traditionally, hummus is prepared with chickpeas, but cannellini beans are a great, healthy alternative that create an ultrasmooth, creamy texture. This White Bean Hummus is full of rich flavors from the warm garlic, fruity olive oil, silky tahini, and bright lemon. Just like traditional chickpea hummus, you can put your own twist on this recipe by blending in your favorite flavors, like caramelized onion, spicy jalapeños, or roasted pine nuts. Pair as a dip with veggies or crackers, or sub for mayonnaise on your favorite sandwich—or even in chicken salad.

DAIRY-FREE, GLUTEN-FREE, VEGAN, UNDER 30 MINUTES, FAMILY FAVORITE

PREP TIME: 5 minutes
BLEND TIME: 45 seconds

1 (15-ounce) can cannellini beans, drained and rinsed

2½ tablespoons tahini

2 tablespoons extra-virgin olive oil

Juice of 2 lemons

2 cloves garlic

½ teaspoon onion powder

Sea salt, to taste

1. Place the cannellini beans, tahini, olive oil, lemon juice, garlic, onion powder, and salt into the blender pitcher in the order listed.

2. Select BLEND, then choose HIGH. Blend for 45 seconds or until the desired consistency is reached.

3. Stored in an airtight container, this keeps in the refrigerator for up to 1 week.

Per serving: Calories: 228; Total fat: 12g; Saturated fat: 2g; Cholesterol: 0mg; Sodium: 277mg; Carbohydrates: 25g; Fiber: 5g; Protein: 6g

Caramelized Onion Dip

SERVES 8

If you can count on me to have Veggies and Lemon-Garlic Whipped Feta Dip (page 63) when you stop by for a get-together, you can also count on me to bring Caramelized Onion Dip when I am invited to a cookout. After all, chips and dip are a staple for any backyard barbecue. Instead of reaching for the onion soup pack, I developed a homemade version for The New Newlywed Cookbook. *This recipe has been modified a bit, plus with the Foodi™ Blender, it is all made in one pitcher! Serve with your favorite potato chips and fresh veggies for the perfect appetizer.*

GLUTEN-FREE, NUT-FREE, VEGETARIAN, UNDER 30 MINUTES, FAMILY FAVORITE

PREP TIME: 5 minutes
COOK TIME: 5 minutes
BLEND TIME: 1 minute

2 tablespoons butter

2 yellow onions, peeled and quartered

1 clove garlic

1 (8-ounce) package cream cheese, quartered

12 ounces sour cream

1 tablespoon fresh thyme

1 teaspoon soy sauce

½ teaspoon onion powder

Sea salt, to taste

Freshly ground black pepper, to taste

Chopped chives, for garnish

1. Place the butter, onions, and garlic in the blender pitcher. Select SAUTÉ.

2. Remove the pitcher lid and let the contents cool for about 5 minutes.

3. Add the cream cheese, sour cream, thyme, soy sauce, onion powder, salt, and pepper into the blender pitcher. PULSE 3 times, then select BLEND then HIGH and run for about 30 seconds, scraping down the sides and repeating until you reach the desired consistency. Serve garnished with the chives.

4. Stored in an airtight container, this keeps in the refrigerator for up to 3 days.

Per serving: *Calories: 210; Total fat: 21g; Saturated fat: 12g; Cholesterol: 60mg; Sodium: 167mg; Carbohydrates: 4g; Fiber: 0g; Protein: 3g*

Beer and Cheese Dip

SERVES 8

A beer hall in Boston known for its giant soft pretzels and dipping sauces has an IPA Cheese Dip on the menu. This Beer and Cheese Dip was inspired by that. Now, I'm not a big soft pretzel fan the way my husband is, but I am a huge cheese fan and I will eat just about anything slathered in this Beer and Cheese Dip. Try serving it with crusty bread, carrot sticks, sliced peppers, and, of course, a giant soft pretzel.

NUT-FREE, VEGETARIAN, 5-INGREDIENT

PREP TIME: 5 minutes
COOK TIME: 30 minutes

VARIATION TIP: For a fun twist on this cheesy dip, add 1 (1-ounce) packet of dry ranch dressing mix to the pitcher along with all of the other ingredients!

1 (8-ounce) package shredded cheddar cheese

1 (8-ounce) package shredded mozzarella cheese

1 (8-ounce) package cream cheese, quartered

1 cup beer, preferably IPA

1 teaspoon garlic salt

1. Place the cheddar cheese, mozzarella, cream cheese, beer, and garlic salt into the blender pitcher in the order listed.

2. Select SAUCE/DIP.

3. Enjoy while warm.

Per serving: *Calories: 206; Total fat: 17g; Saturated fat: 10g; Cholesterol: 57mg; Sodium: 339mg; Carbohydrates: 2g; Fiber: 0g; Protein: 8g*

Buffalo Chicken Dip

SERVES 8

This recipe is a must-make for your next game night or football party. Whether you're watching the game from home or prepping snacks to tailgate, there is no more quintessential football food than Buffalo Chicken Dip. Serve with tortilla chips, carrot sticks, and celery stalks.

GLUTEN-FREE, NUT-FREE, FAMILY FAVORITE, 5-INGREDIENT

PREP TIME: 5 minutes
COOK TIME: 30 minutes

2 cups cooked chicken breast, chopped

1 (8-ounce) package cream cheese, quartered

¾ cup Buffalo sauce

¾ cup ranch dressing

1 cup shredded Colby–Monterey Jack cheese

1. Place the chicken, cream cheese, Buffalo sauce, ranch dressing, and cheese into the blender pitcher in the order listed.

2. Select SAUCE/DIP.

3. This can be made in advance and stored in an airtight container in the refrigerator for up to 3 days.

Per serving: *Calories: 319; Total fat: 27g; Saturated fat: 11g; Cholesterol: 83mg; Sodium: 1242mg; Carbohydrates: 3g; Fiber: 0g; Protein: 16g*

Bacon and Spinach Artichoke Dip

SERVES 8

Whether served hot or cold, spinach dip is welcome at any get-together. While a regular blender can be used to whip up spinach, cream cheese, and mayo for a creamy cold dip, I prefer a hot spinach artichoke dip full of melty cheese. This version is an amped-up version of my original, thanks to a not-so-secret ingredient: bacon! Just a few slices of bacon, sautéed with garlic before cooking, together with the remaining ingredients, imparts smoky flavor throughout each bite. Serve this decadent dip with veggies, tortilla chips, or crackers and enjoy!

GLUTEN-FREE, NUT-FREE, FAMILY FAVORITE

PREP TIME: 10 minutes
COOK TIME: 35 minutes

SUBSTITUTION TIP: If you have fresh spinach on hand, you can use fresh spinach in place of frozen. Make sure you steam and blanch the spinach in ice water, squeeze out the excess liquid, and chop to achieve the same texture as the frozen variety.

2 slices bacon, chopped

2 cloves garlic, minced

1 (14-ounce) can artichoke hearts, drained

1 (10-ounce) package frozen spinach, thawed and drained

1 (8-ounce) package cream cheese, quartered

¼ cup sour cream

1 (8-ounce) package shredded mozzarella cheese

¼ teaspoon red pepper flakes

½ teaspoon sea salt

1. Place the bacon and garlic into the blender pitcher. Select SAUTÉ.

2. Add the artichoke hearts, spinach, cream cheese, sour cream, mozzarella cheese, red pepper flakes, and salt into the blender pitcher.

3. Select SAUCE/DIP.

4. Enjoy while warm.

Per serving: *Calories: 270; Total fat: 23g; Saturated fat: 10g; Cholesterol: 58mg; Sodium: 606mg; Carbohydrates: 9g; Fiber: 3g; Protein: 12g*

Creamy Tomato Soup, *page 74*

5

Soups

Creamy Tomato Soup

SERVES 4

This Creamy Tomato Soup recipe warms you up from the inside out. This version is ultra-creamy and full of flavor. Whether I am feeling under the weather or I had a lousy day, a bowl of hot soup and a grilled cheese sandwich always makes me feel better. If you want to get extra fancy, cut a grilled cheese sandwich into cubes on top of your soup!

GLUTEN-FREE, NUT-FREE, VEGETARIAN, FAMILY FAVORITE

PREP TIME: 10 minutes
COOK TIME: 35 minutes

SUBSTITUTION TIP:
I prefer micro basil, but if you can't find it, you can substitute roughly chopped basil in a pinch.

3 tablespoons unsalted butter

1 yellow onion, peeled and quartered

2 garlic cloves

2 tablespoons tomato paste

1 (28-ounce) can whole tomatoes

1 cup vegetable broth

⅓ cup heavy cream

1 tablespoon brown sugar

½ teaspoon sea salt

Sour cream, for garnish (optional)

Micro basil, for garnish (optional)

1. Place the butter, onion, garlic, and tomato paste into the blender pitcher. Select SAUTÉ.

2. Add the whole tomatoes, vegetable broth, heavy cream, brown sugar, and salt to the blender pitcher, then select SMOOTH SOUP.

3. Top with a dollop of sour cream and basil, if using.

Per serving: Calories: 291; Total fat: 25g; Saturated fat: 16g; Cholesterol: 84mg; Sodium: 193mg; Carbohydrates: 16g; Fiber: 3g; Protein: 3g

Black Bean Soup

Canned beans are one of my favorite ingredients because they are super easy, full of flavor, nutritious, and inexpensive. Whether you are looking for a hearty, Meatless Monday meal that is still full of protein, or a flavorful lunch option that can be packed and reheated, I have the recipe for you! This Black Bean Soup is delicious if you follow the recipe as it's written, but if you really want to put it over the top, pile on sliced avocado, chopped fresh tomato, and a sprinkle of roasted corn.

DAIRY-FREE, GLUTEN-FREE, NUT-FREE, VEGAN

PREP TIME: 5 minutes
COOK TIME: 35 minutes

DID YOU KNOW?: In order to build the most flavor throughout the recipes in this book, I opted to leverage the SAUTÉ program as a first step to cook the onions and garlic. While this adds a nice depth of flavor to the recipe, you may choose to skip this step if you are short on time.

1 tablespoon extra-virgin olive oil

1 yellow onion, peeled and quartered

3 garlic cloves

2 (15-ounce) cans black beans, drained and rinsed

3 cups vegetable broth

1 jalapeño, stemmed, cored (remove seeds and membrane), and chopped

1 teaspoon ground cumin

1 teaspoon chili powder

½ teaspoon ground coriander

¼ teaspoon sea salt

¼ teaspoon freshly ground black pepper

¼ teaspoon cayenne pepper (optional)

Sour cream, for garnish (optional)

Fresh cilantro, chopped for garnish

1. Place the olive oil, onion, and garlic into the blender pitcher. Select SAUTÉ.

2. Add the black beans, vegetable broth, jalapeño, cumin, chili powder, coriander, salt, pepper, and cayenne (if using) to the blender pitcher, then select HEARTY SOUP.

3. Garnish with cilantro and sour cream (if using), and serve.

Per serving: *Calories: 227; Total fat: 4g; Saturated fat: 1g; Cholesterol: 0mg; Sodium: 181mg; Carbohydrates: 36g; Fiber: 13g; Protein: 12g*

Butternut Squash Soup with Pomegranate Seeds

SERVES 4

Cuddle up on a cold evening with a warm bowl of butternut squash soup! Comforting and delicious, I love the velvety creaminess of this soup. The sweetness of the butternut squash and warmth of the nutmeg play perfectly together for a bowl full of cozy.

GLUTEN-FREE, NUT-FREE, VEGETARIAN

PREP TIME: 10 minutes
COOK TIME: 35 minutes

HACK IT: Fresh butternut squash should be peeled and seeded. For easier prep, cubed butternut squash is often sold pre-chopped in the refrigerated case of the produce section. You can also use frozen squash in this recipe.

2 tablespoons butter

1 yellow onion, peeled and quartered

1½ pounds (24 ounces) butternut squash, cubed

2¼ cups vegetable stock

1 tablespoon brown sugar

¼ teaspoon dried thyme

⅛ teaspoon ground nutmeg

Sea salt, to taste

Sour cream, for garnish

Pomegranate seeds, for garnish

Fresh sage leaves, for garnish

1. Place the butter and onion into the blender pitcher. Select SAUTÉ.

2. Add the butternut squash, vegetable stock, brown sugar, thyme, nutmeg, and salt to the blender pitcher, then select SMOOTH SOUP.

3. Top with a drizzle of sour cream, pomegranate seeds, and fresh sage.

Per serving: Calories: 152; Total fat: 6g; Saturated fat: 4g; Cholesterol: 15mg; Sodium: 144mg; Carbohydrates: 26g; Fiber: 4g; Protein: 2g

Creamy Carrot-Ginger Soup

SERVES 4

Sometimes the simplest recipes become overly complicated with the addition of too many ingredients. In this soup, the carrot is the star. I kept from adding extra fruits and veggies that would overpower the flavor of the carrot. Instead, I focused only on ingredients that complement versus complicate: sautéed onion adds depth of flavor, while the butter and coconut milk add to the silky texture. Ginger is the final addition, providing a zing that perfectly plays off the carrot's earthy sweetness. Enjoy!

GLUTEN-FREE, NUT-FREE, VEGAN

PREP TIME: 10 minutes
COOK TIME: 35 minutes

HACK IT: I love using fresh ginger in recipes and always keep a knob in my refrigerator. To easily remove the skin of the ginger, use the back of a spoon to get into the nooks and crannies.

2 tablespoons unsalted butter

1 yellow onion, peeled and quartered

3 carrots, peeled and chopped

2 tablespoons minced ginger

2 cups vegetable broth

¼ cup full-fat coconut milk

Sea salt, to taste

Freshly ground black pepper, to taste

Sunflower seeds or pepitas, for garnish (optional)

1. Place the butter and onion into the blender pitcher. Select SAUTÉ.

2. Add the carrots, ginger, vegetable broth, coconut milk, salt, and pepper to the blender pitcher, then select SMOOTH SOUP.

Per serving: *Calories: 121; Total fat: 9g; Saturated fat: 6g; Cholesterol: 15mg; Sodium: 107mg; Carbohydrates: 10g; Fiber: 3g; Protein: 1g*

Pumpkin Soup

SERVES 4

This comforting soup is like wrapping yourself up in your favorite fuzzy sweater! Packed with the flavors of fall, this Pumpkin Soup is best enjoyed on a chilly night. I love how the sweet sugar and warming pumpkin pie spice play together. If you are entertaining, try serving this soup in hollowed-out mini pumpkins and your guests are sure to be impressed.

GLUTEN-FREE, NUT-FREE, VEGETARIAN

PREP TIME: 10 minutes
COOK TIME: 35 minutes

SUBSTITUTION TIP: I like using pumpkin purée in this recipe because it is always available. In the fall when fresh pumpkin is in season, swap out the pumpkin purée with 2 cups chopped fresh pumpkin.

2 tablespoons butter

1 yellow onion, peeled and quartered

1 (15-ounce) can pumpkin purée

2¼ cups vegetable stock

1 tablespoon brown sugar

¼ teaspoon dried thyme

⅛ teaspoon pumpkin pie spice

Sea salt, to taste

Sour cream, for garnish

Pepitas, for garnish

1. Place the butter and onion into the blender pitcher. Select SAUTÉ.

2. Add the pumpkin purée, vegetable stock, brown sugar, thyme, pumpkin pie spice, and salt to the blender pitcher, then select SMOOTH SOUP.

3. Garnish with a dollop of sour cream and pepitas.

Per serving: Calories: 141; Total fat: 6g; Saturated fat: 4g; Cholesterol: 15mg; Sodium: 127mg; Carbohydrates: 21g; Fiber: 6g; Protein: 2g

Red Lentil Soup with Toasted Cumin Seeds

SERVES 4

Whether you are vegetarian, or just trying to eat less meat, this creamy Red Lentil Soup is an easy meat-free meal. And it comes together in less than an hour from start to finish! Enjoy with a side salad or serve over steamed rice. Add a squeeze of fresh lemon on top and dig in!

GLUTEN-FREE, NUT-FREE, VEGETARIAN

PREP TIME: 10 minutes
COOK TIME: 35 minutes

HACK IT: Use the SAUTÉ program to toast nuts and seeds, like cumin seeds, for garnish. Note that this program will not only toast the nuts and seeds—it will also chop them!

1 tablespoon extra-virgin olive oil

1 yellow onion, peeled and quartered

1 tablespoon tomato paste

4 cups vegetable broth

1¼ cups red lentils, rinsed

1 tablespoon lemon juice

2 teaspoons ground cumin

1 teaspoon paprika

¼ teaspoon cayenne pepper

¼ teaspoon sea salt

Greek yogurt, for garnish

Toasted cumin seeds, for garnish

1. Place the olive oil, onion, and tomato paste into the blender pitcher. Select SAUTÉ.

2. Add the vegetable broth, red lentils, lemon juice, cumin, paprika, cayenne pepper, and salt to the blender pitcher in the order listed. Select SMOOTH SOUP.

3. Garnish with Greek yogurt and toasted cumin seeds and enjoy warm.

Per serving: Calories: 266; Total fat: 5g; Saturated fat: 1g; Cholesterol: 0mg; Sodium: 270mg; Carbohydrates: 42g; Fiber: 8g; Protein: 15g

Rosemary and Lemon White Bean Minestrone Soup

More of an equation than a recipe, minestrone soup is considered a kitchen-sink recipe. Basically, you can use whatever ingredients you have to build this soup. Toss together fresh herbs, fresh greens, and any canned beans from the cupboard, and you magically have a delicious meal. This version is my go-to because I love the combination of floral rosemary and bright, citrusy lemon.

GLUTEN-FREE, NUT-FREE, VEGETARIAN

PREP TIME: 10 minutes
COOK TIME: 35 minutes

2 tablespoons olive oil

1 yellow onion, peeled and quartered

2 cloves garlic, peeled

2 celery stalks

2 sprigs fresh rosemary, stripped

4 cups vegetable stock

1 lemon, zested and juiced

1 cup kale leaves, roughly chopped

⅓ cup grated Parmesan cheese

½ teaspoon sea salt

¼ teaspoon ground black pepper

1 (15-ounce) can cannellini beans, drained

1. Place the olive oil, onion, and garlic into the blender pitcher. Select SAUTÉ.

2. Add the celery, rosemary, vegetable stock, lemon zest and juice, kale, Parmesan, salt, and pepper to the blender pitcher in the order listed. Select HEARTY SOUP.

3. With 6 minutes remaining on the program, add the cannellini beans.

Per serving: *Calories: 192; Total fat: 6g; Saturated fat: 2g; Cholesterol: 7mg; Sodium: 446mg; Carbohydrates: 25g; Fiber: 7g; Protein: 10g*

Winter Vegetable and Barley Soup

Like many of the soup recipes throughout this chapter, the key to this Winter Vegetable and Barley Soup is building a flavorful broth base. Sautéing the onion and garlic builds flavors that are impossible to achieve in other blenders that claim to heat ingredients through friction. Along with the broth, the vegetables are cooked until tender, and the barley helps to finish off this hearty soup.

DAIRY-FREE, GLUTEN-FREE, NUT-FREE, VEGAN

PREP TIME: 10 minutes
COOK TIME: 35 minutes

2 tablespoons extra-virgin olive oil

1 yellow onion, peeled and quartered

2 garlic cloves

3 cups vegetable broth

2 medium carrots, peeled and chopped

2 celery stalks, chopped

1 teaspoon fresh thyme

1 (15-ounce) can diced tomatoes

1 tablespoon gluten-free soy sauce

1 cup kale leaves, roughly chopped

¼ cup quick-cooking barley

2 tablespoons chopped fresh parsley, for serving

1. Place the olive oil, onion, and garlic into the blender pitcher. Select SAUTÉ.

2. Add the broth, carrots, celery, thyme, diced tomatoes, soy sauce, and kale to the blender pitcher in the order listed. Select HEARTY SOUP.

3. With 20 minutes remaining on the program, add the barley.

4. Garnish with parsley and serve.

Per serving: Calories: 170; Total fat: 7g; Saturated fat: 1g; Cholesterol: 0mg; Sodium: 458mg; Carbohydrates: 24g; Fiber: 5g; Protein: 4g

Potato-Leek Soup

Hearty and luscious, this Potato-Leek Soup is comfort food at its finest. I love the mild flavor of leeks and how perfectly it pairs with potatoes. If you haven't worked with leeks before, be sure to clean them thoroughly, as dirt tends to get trapped between the layers. Cut off the root ends and trim off the tough green tops, leaving only the light green and white sections, then slice the leeks in half lengthwise and wash or soak them to remove any dirt, before slicing as directed. Sautéing the leeks first will help bring out their flavor, similar to sautéing an onion. Before serving, add a bit of hot sauce for a kick or serve topped with crispy, buttery croutons for an added crunch.

GLUTEN-FREE, NUT-FREE, VEGETARIAN

PREP TIME: 10 minutes
COOK TIME: 35 minutes

SUBSTITUTION TIP: If you are dairy-free but want to try this recipe, replace the butter with olive oil and replace the heavy whipping cream with canned coconut milk.

1 tablespoon butter

1 large leek, rinsed, trimmed, and sliced

2 cloves garlic

2 medium russet potatoes, peeled and roughly chopped

3 cups vegetable stock

¾ teaspoon dried thyme

½ teaspoon salt

½ cup heavy whipping cream

½ teaspoon pepper

Chopped chives, for garnish

1. Place butter, leek, and garlic into the blender pitcher. Select SAUTÉ.

2. Add the potatoes, vegetable stock, thyme, and salt to the blender pitcher, then select SMOOTH SOUP.

3. Once the program has completed, carefully remove the lid and stir in the whipping cream and pepper.

4. Garnish with chives and serve warm.

Per serving: Calories: 239; Total fat: 14g; Saturated fat: 9g; Cholesterol: 48mg; Sodium: 272mg; Carbohydrates: 26g; Fiber: 3g; Protein: 3g

Cajun Corn Chowder

SERVES 4

This recipe screams summer but surprisingly uses frozen corn kernels versus fresh corn on the cob. Not only are frozen corn kernels perfect for this recipe because they cook through and break down to provide a bit of starch to thicken the chowder, but the corn is also frozen at the peak of freshness, so you can enjoy this recipe year-round.

GLUTEN-FREE, NUT-FREE, VEGETARIAN

PREP TIME: 10 minutes
COOK TIME: 35 minutes

VARIATION TIP: Try adding andouille sausage or kielbasa to this recipe for added smokiness. Simply give the sausage a rough chop and add it to the pitcher in step 2.

2 tablespoons unsalted butter

1 yellow onion, peeled and quartered

2 cloves garlic

3 cups frozen corn kernels

1 red potato, chopped

2½ cups vegetable broth

¼ cup heavy cream

¼ teaspoon sea salt

¼ teaspoon freshly ground black pepper

¼ teaspoon Cajun seasoning

2 tablespoons minced fresh parsley, for garnish

1. Place the butter, onion, and garlic into the blender pitcher. Select SAUTÉ.

2. Add the corn, potato, vegetable broth, heavy cream, salt, pepper, and Cajun seasoning to the blender pitcher, then select HEARTY SOUP.

3. Garnish with parsley and serve.

Per serving: *Calories: 253; Total fat: 13g; Saturated fat: 7g; Cholesterol: 35mg; Sodium: 260mg; Carbohydrates: 35g; Fiber: 5g; Protein: 5g*

Lobster Bisque

SERVES 4

One of my favorite things about working at Ninja® are the people I work with. Not only are they incredibly intelligent, but they are super creative as well! While developing new products, we are all encouraged to take them home and cook—and I love seeing what people come up with. When the Foodi™ Blender came in, one of the women on my team was telling me about the Lobster Bisque she made, and I was blown away by her courage to try a bisque in the blender. The recipe was a success, and I am happy she shared it with me so that I can pass it along to all of you. Thank you, Gretchen!

GLUTEN-FREE, NUT-FREE

PREP TIME: 10 minutes
COOK TIME: 30 minutes

VARIATION TIP: For a thicker bisque base, reduce the amount of seafood stock down to as little as 1 cup.

3 tablespoons butter

2 cloves garlic

1 yellow onion, peeled and quartered

2 cups seafood stock

1 teaspoon fresh thyme

½ teaspoon cayenne pepper

1 teaspoon Old Bay seasoning

1 cup heavy cream

2 fresh lobster tails, lobster meat removed and cut into 1½-inch pieces

1. Place the butter, garlic, onion, seafood stock, thyme, cayenne, Old Bay seasoning, heavy cream, and lobster meat into the blender pitcher in the order listed.

2. Select HEARTY SOUP.

Per serving: *Calories: 377; Total fat: 32g; Saturated fat: 19g; Cholesterol: 172mg; Sodium: 414mg; Carbohydrates: 5g; Fiber: 0g; Protein: 17g*

Broccoli-Cheddar Soup

SERVES 4

There are so many variations of broccoli and cheese soup, but for such a basic dish I have always felt the recipes were overly complicated. This version comes together easily on busy weeknights because it takes just over 30 minutes, start to finish. All you need to do is toss the ingredients in the blender in the order listed and you are sure to have a cheesy and delicious dish!

GLUTEN-FREE, NUT-FREE, VEGETARIAN, FAMILY FAVORITE

PREP TIME: 10 minutes
COOK TIME: 35 minutes

VARIATION TIP: I prefer my Broccoli-Cheddar Soup with some texture, so the HEARTY SOUP program achieves the perfect texture for me. If you prefer a smooth, puréed texture, simply choose SMOOTH SOUP instead.

2 tablespoons unsalted butter

1 yellow onion, peeled and quartered

1 cup carrots, diced

2 cups vegetable broth

1 head broccoli, trimmed into 1½-inch florets

½ teaspoon thyme

½ teaspoon garlic powder

1½ cups heavy cream

1 cup shredded sharp cheddar cheese, plus more for garnish

⅓ cup grated Parmesan cheese

1. Place the butter, onion, and carrots into the blender pitcher. Select SAUTÉ.

2. Add the vegetable broth, broccoli, thyme, and garlic powder to the blender pitcher, then select HEARTY SOUP.

3. With about 10 minutes remaining in the program, add the heavy cream, cheddar cheese, and Parmesan cheese.

4. Garnish with additional cheddar cheese and serve.

Per serving: *Calories: 578; Total fat: 51g; Saturated fat: 32g; Cholesterol: 174mg; Sodium: 672mg; Carbohydrates: 18g; Fiber: 4g; Protein: 16g*

Ginger-Garlic Chicken Ramen

SERVES 2

Some folks may turn up their noses at packaged dried ramen, but any cook worth their salt knows that those noodles are perfect for homemade ramen. What sets this Ginger-Garlic Chicken Ramen apart from the kind you make in the microwave? We ditch the seasoning pack and build the broth right in the Foodi™ Blender. Warm ginger and garlic flavor the broth while the chicken cooks. Then, stir in the greens and dried noodles and you will have made a delicious bowl of ramen in less than an hour start to finish.

DAIRY-FREE, NUT-FREE, FAMILY FAVORITE

PREP TIME: 10 minutes
COOK TIME: 35 minutes

1 tablespoon extra-virgin olive oil

1 shallot, peeled, cut in 1-inch pieces

4 garlic cloves

2 teaspoons fresh ginger

1 cup uncooked boneless, skinless chicken thighs, cut in 1-inch pieces

1 bunch green onions, thinly sliced, green and white parts, divided

4 cups chicken stock

1 teaspoon toasted sesame oil

1 (3-ounce) package dried ramen, seasoning pack discarded

2 baby bok choy heads, separated into leaves

1. Place the olive oil, shallot, garlic, and ginger into the blender pitcher. Select SAUTÉ.

2. Add the chicken, green onions, chicken stock, and sesame oil to the blender pitcher in the order listed. Select HEARTY SOUP.

3. With 3 minutes remaining in the program, add the ramen noodles and baby bok choy.

4. When the program is complete, check to make sure the internal temperature of the chicken is 165ºF.

Per serving: Calories: 379; Total fat: 21g; Saturated fat: 3g; Cholesterol: 80mg; Sodium: 392mg; Carbohydrates: 23g; Fiber: 4g; Protein: 22g

Chicken Tortilla Soup

SERVES 4

If you love Tex-Mex as much as I do, this Mexican-inspired Chicken Tortilla Soup is a must-add to your rotation. Packed with bold spices and whole ingredients, this is my favorite way to do a guilt-free Tex-Mex Tuesday. Like a traditional tortilla soup, this version is—of course—served topped with crispy fried tortilla strips for a delightful crunch. You can also add fresh avocado, sour cream, and pico de gallo.

DAIRY-FREE, GLUTEN-FREE, NUT-FREE, FAMILY FAVORITE

PREP TIME: 10 minutes
COOK TIME: 35 minutes

1 tablespoon extra-virgin olive oil

1 onion, peeled and quartered

2 garlic cloves

2 teaspoons tomato paste

4 cups chicken stock

1 cup frozen corn kernels

1 cup uncooked chicken breast, cut in 1-inch pieces

1 jalapeño, stemmed, cored (remove seeds and membrane), and chopped

½ teaspoon ground cumin

¼ teaspoon sea salt

¼ teaspoon freshly ground black pepper

1 (15-ounce) can pinto beans, drained and rinsed

Fresh cilantro, chopped, for garnish

Tortilla strips, for serving

1. Place the olive oil, onion, garlic, and tomato paste into the blender pitcher. Select SAUTÉ.

2. Add the chicken stock, corn kernels, chicken, jalapeño, cumin, salt, and pepper to the blender pitcher in the order listed. Select HEARTY SOUP.

3. With 6 minutes remaining in the program, add the pinto beans.

4. When the program is complete, check to make sure the internal temperature of the chicken is 165°F. Garnish with cilantro and tortilla strips and serve.

Per serving: *Calories: 240; Total fat: 6g; Saturated fat: 1g; Cholesterol: 16mg; Sodium: 101mg; Carbohydrates: 31g; Fiber: 8g; Protein: 19g*

Bacon-Cauliflower Soup

I have learned a lot since I first started developing recipes, and I like to think that, with each cookbook I work on, I improve as both a cook and an author. However, when polling friends and family for recipes to adapt and develop for the Foodi™ blender, this recipe from my first cookbook continued to rise to the top. In fact, despite writing seven cookbooks and developing hundreds of recipes, it ranks as one of my most popular. So here I give you my creamy and delicious Bacon-Cauliflower Soup—reinvented for the Foodi Blender.

GLUTEN-FREE, NUT-FREE, FAMILY FAVORITE

PREP TIME: 10 minutes
COOK TIME: 35 minutes

VARIATION TIP: This soup was developed as a dairy-free, Paleo-friendly option for folks who love a loaded baked potato soup. For a little variety, try topping a bowl of this soup with a garnish of shredded cheddar cheese and crispy bacon.

1 tablespoon butter

2 bacon slices, chopped

1 yellow onion, peeled and quartered

½ teaspoon garlic powder

1 head cauliflower, trimmed into florets

3 cups chicken broth

⅓ cup full-fat coconut milk

1 teaspoon sea salt

1 teaspoon freshly ground black pepper

1. Place the butter, bacon, and onion into the blender pitcher. Select SAUTÉ.

2. Add the garlic powder, cauliflower, chicken broth, coconut milk, salt, and pepper to the blender pitcher, then select SMOOTH SOUP.

Per serving: *Calories: 238; Total fat: 15g; Saturated fat: 8g; Cholesterol: 33mg; Sodium: 1238mg; Carbohydrates: 17g; Fiber: 7g; Protein: 10g*

Red Raspberry
Dressing, *page 100*

6

Dressings and Sauces

Red Raspberry Dressing

MAKES 1½ CUPS

I love a bold dressing, but I usually opt for something savory over sweet. This Red Raspberry Dressing completely changed my mind. It's fruity and sweet, and I love to whip it up in the summer when raspberries are ripe and bursting with flavor. Drizzle it on top of a spinach salad topped with grilled chicken or any other salad that could use a bright pop of color and bold raspberry flavor!

DAIRY-FREE, GLUTEN-FREE, NUT-FREE, VEGAN, UNDER 30 MINUTES

PREP TIME: 5 minutes
BLEND TIME: 1 minute

SUBSTITUTION TIP: Use frozen raspberries if you can't find fresh ones. Your dressing will turn out a bit thicker, so allow it to come to room temperature for 10 to 15 minutes before serving.

1½ cups fresh raspberries
½ cup extra-virgin olive oil
¼ cup red wine vinegar
1 garlic clove

1 teaspoon Dijon mustard
Sea salt, to taste
Freshly ground black pepper, to taste

1. Place the raspberries, olive oil, red wine vinegar, garlic, Dijon mustard, salt, and pepper into the blender pitcher in the order listed.

2. Select BLEND, then choose HIGH. Blend for 1 minute, or until the desired consistency is reached.

3. Store in an airtight container and refrigerate for up to 1 week.

Per serving (2 tablespoons): Calories: 89; Total fat: 9g; Saturated fat: 1g; Cholesterol: 0g; Sodium: 5g; Carbohydrates: 2g; Fiber: 1g; Protein: 0g

Cauliflower Alfredo Sauce

I got my start in food when I decided to go Paleo and had to teach myself how to cook in order to enjoy the foods I loved on a diet that excluded dairy and grains. Although I have reintroduced these ingredients back into my diet, I am constantly asked for Paleo, dairy-free, and gluten-free recipes—especially recipes that will cure a craving for Italian! Needless to say, cauliflower is the solution for many of my dairy-free and gluten-free recipes. For example, in lieu of heavy cream, butter, and cheese, this Cauliflower Alfredo Sauce gets its creamy texture from puréed cauliflower and makes a great veggie-filled alternative on top of your pastas or veggies. If you want the sauce a little bit thinner, add a few tablespoons of veggie stock.

DAIRY-FREE, GLUTEN-FREE, NUT-FREE, VEGAN, 5-INGREDIENT

PREP TIME: 10 minutes
COOK TIME: 35 minutes

VARIATION TIP: If you are not dairy-free and are simply using this recipe to sneak more veggies into your diet, I recommend adding anywhere between ½ to 1 cup Parmesan cheese to this recipe to add some additional saltiness!

1 tablespoon extra-virgin olive oil

3 garlic cloves

1 small head cauliflower, trimmed into 1½-inch florets

1½ cups water

½ teaspoon sea salt

¼ teaspoon freshly ground black pepper

1. Place the oil and garlic into the blender pitcher. Select SAUTÉ.

2. Add the cauliflower florets, water, salt, and pepper, and select SAUCE/DIP.

3. Store in an airtight container and refrigerate for 3 or 4 days.

Per serving (½ cup): *Calories: 20; Total fat: 0g; Saturated fat: 0g; Cholesterol: 0mg; Sodium: 66mg; Carbohydrates: 2g; Fiber: 1g; Protein: 1g*

Avocado and Cilantro Dressing

MAKES 1½ CUPS

This creamy Avocado and Cilantro Dressing is a great alternative to some other creamy dressings that are loaded with calories. Not only does it add a punch of flavor and creaminess to any salad, but I also love to use this recipe as a marinade for chicken and as a dipping sauce alongside a veggie platter.

GLUTEN-FREE, NUT-FREE, VEGETARIAN, UNDER 30 MINUTES

PREP TIME: 5 minutes
BLEND TIME: 1 minute

HACK IT: If you're looking for a thinner dressing, add more water, 1 tablespoon at a time, and PULSE until you've achieved your ideal consistency.

1 avocado, peeled and pitted
2 cups cilantro leaves
½ cup plain Greek yogurt
½ cup water
2 cloves garlic
2 teaspoons lime juice
1 teaspoon salt

1. Place the avocado, cilantro, Greek yogurt, water, garlic, lime juice, and salt into the blender pitcher in the order listed.

2. Select BLEND, then choose HIGH. Blend for 1 minute, or until the desired consistency is reached.

3. Store in an airtight container and refrigerate for up to 1 week.

Per serving (2 tablespoons): Calories: 27; Total fat: 2g; Saturated fat: 0g; Cholesterol: 1mg; Sodium: 201mg; Carbohydrates: 2g; Fiber: 1g; Protein: 1g

Carrot-Ginger Dressing

MAKES 1½ CUPS

We recently went to a hibachi dinner with our friends Alex and Maddison and spent about 30 minutes breaking down the ingredients in the dressing on the house salad and reviewing our favorite ginger dressing recipes. (One may say we have too much time on our hands, but those who know us know we just love food!) Well, I am here to set the record straight: This is the recipe we came up with for the ultimate Carrot-Ginger Dressing. Serve over fresh, crisp iceberg lettuce.

DAIRY-FREE, GLUTEN-FREE, VEGETARIAN, UNDER 30 MINUTES

PREP TIME: 5 minutes
BLEND TIME: 1 minute

SUBSTITUTION TIP: Use agave syrup in place of honey to make this recipe vegan.

½ cup extra-virgin olive oil
½ cup rice vinegar
2 large carrots, peeled and halved
2 tablespoons ginger, peeled and roughly chopped
Juice of 2 limes
1½ tablespoons honey
1½ teaspoons sesame oil
Sea salt, to taste

1. Place the olive oil, rice vinegar, carrots, ginger, lime juice, honey, sesame oil, and salt into the blender pitcher in the order listed.

2. Select BLEND, then choose HIGH. Blend for 1 minute, or until the desired consistency is reached.

3. Store in an airtight container and refrigerate for up to 1 week.

Per serving (2 tablespoons): *Calories: 272; Total fat: 29g; Saturated fat: 4g; Cholesterol: 0mg; Sodium: 9mg; Carbohydrates: 4g; Fiber: 0g; Protein: 0g*

Creamy Lemon Vinaigrette

MAKES 1 CUP

A classic vinaigrette is made by mixing oil with something acidic, like lemon juice. The Greek yogurt makes this version extra creamy. Tangy and delicious, it elevates any dish, whether it is used as a dressing or marinade. Enjoy it as a simple, effortless dressing to top off your favorite salad or drizzle it over fish. This Creamy Lemon Vinaigrette is sure to brighten any dish.

GLUTEN-FREE, NUT-FREE, VEGETARIAN, UNDER 30 MINUTES

PREP TIME: 5 minutes
BLEND TIME: 1 minute

¼ **cup plain Greek yogurt**

Juice of 2 lemons

Zest of 1 lemon

2 tablespoons extra-virgin olive oil

½ **shallot**

2 teaspoons honey

Sea salt, to taste

Freshly ground black pepper, to taste

1. Place the Greek yogurt, lemon juice and zest, olive oil, shallot, honey, salt, and pepper into the blender pitcher in the order listed.

2. Select BLEND, then choose LOW. Blend for 1 minute, or until the desired consistency is reached.

3. Store in an airtight container and refrigerate for up to 1 week.

Per serving (2 tablespoons): Calories: 43; Total fat: 4g; Saturated fat: 1g; Cholesterol: 1mg; Sodium: 16mg; Carbohydrates: 3g; Fiber: 0g; Protein: 0g

Caesar Dressing

MAKES 1½ CUPS

I am a big fan of making salad dressing at home. While store-bought dressings are definitely convenient, whizzing up your own in the blender only takes a few minutes, you control the ingredients, and the flavor is unparalleled. We are definitely a Caesar Salad house, so this recipe is always on repeat.

GLUTEN-FREE, NUT-FREE, UNDER 30 MINUTES, FAMILY FAVORITE

PREP TIME: 5 minutes
BLEND TIME: 1 minute

SUBSTITUTION TIP: Can't find anchovy paste at your local grocery store? Buy anchovy fillets instead, and use 2 fillets to equal 1 teaspoon of paste.

2 garlic cloves

1 teaspoon anchovy paste

Juice of 1 lemon

1¼ cups mayonnaise

1½ teaspoons Dijon mustard

1½ teaspoons Worcestershire sauce

½ cup grated Parmigiano-Reggiano cheese

Sea salt, to taste

Freshly ground black pepper, to taste

1. Place the garlic, anchovy paste, lemon juice, mayonnaise, Dijon mustard, Worcestershire sauce, cheese, salt, and pepper into the blender pitcher in the order listed.

2. Select BLEND, then choose MED. Blend for 1 minute, or until the desired consistency is reached.

3. Store in an airtight container and refrigerate for up to 1 week.

Per serving (2 tablespoons): Calories: 119; Total fat: 10g; Saturated fat: 2g; Cholesterol: 11mg; Sodium: 265mg; Carbohydrates: 7g; Fiber: 0g; Protein: 2g

Roasted Red Pepper Dressing

MAKES 1½ CUPS

This Roasted Red Pepper Dressing is as flavorful as it is bright! It makes a great addition to a green salad piled high with veggies, but, like most of the dressings in this book, it also tastes delicious drizzled on chicken or salmon. You can either use the dressing immediately or store in a jar in the refrigerator for up to a week.

DAIRY-FREE, GLUTEN-FREE, NUT-FREE, VEGAN, UNDER 30 MINUTES

PREP TIME: 5 minutes
BLEND TIME: 1 minute

SUBSTITUTION TIP:
Don't have parsley on hand? Try basil or chives in its place.

1 cup roasted red peppers, drained
¼ cup apple cider vinegar
¼ cup water
¼ cup extra-virgin olive oil
2 cloves garlic
2 tablespoons agave syrup
2 tablespoons parsley
Sea salt, to taste
Freshly ground black pepper, to taste

1. Place the roasted red peppers, apple cider vinegar, water, olive oil, garlic, agave syrup, parsley, salt, and pepper into the blender pitcher in the order listed.

2. Select BLEND, then choose MED. Blend for 1 minute, or until the desired consistency is reached.

Per serving: Calories: 55; Total fat: 5g; Saturated fat: 1g; Cholesterol: 0mg; Sodium: 1mg; Carbohydrates: 4g; Fiber: 0g; Protein: 0g

Spicy Peanut Sauce

MAKES 1½ CUPS

The best sauces are incredibly versatile and can be used as a dressing, marinade, or sauce. This Spicy Peanut Sauce is no different—it can instantly turn just about any ingredients into a meal. My favorite way to use this is as a simmer sauce. Once the sauce is blended together, add it to a pan with chicken, fresh veggies, and noodles for a filling and tasty dish.

DAIRY-FREE, VEGAN, UNDER 30 MINUTES, FAMILY FAVORITE

PREP TIME: 5 minutes
BLEND TIME: 1 minute

HACK IT: There's no need to purchase special peanut butter for this recipe, just use what you have in the pantry—crunchy or smooth both work well!

¾ cup peanut butter

¼ cup soy sauce

2 tablespoons sesame oil

3 cloves garlic

1 tablespoon fresh ginger, peeled

1 jalapeño, stemmed, cored (remove seeds and membrane), and chopped

2 teaspoons sriracha

¼ cup water

1. Place the peanut butter, soy sauce, sesame oil, garlic, ginger, jalapeño, sriracha, and water into the blender pitcher in the order listed.

2. Select BLEND, then choose HIGH. Blend for 1 minute, or until the desired consistency is reached.

3. Store in an airtight container and refrigerate for 3 or 4 days.

Per serving (¼ cup): Calories: 250; Total fat: 21g; Saturated fat: 5g; Cholesterol: 0mg; Sodium: 710mg; Carbohydrates: 8g; Fiber: 2g; Protein: 11g

Mole Sauce

Don't be intimidated by the list of ingredients; many of these ingredients are everyday spices you are sure to have in the pantry. This sauce comes together quickly, but was inspired by the flavors of a traditional Mexican mole that takes hours to prepare on the stove. Enjoy this version drizzled on tacos, enchiladas, burritos, nachos, veggies, and pretty much anything else you can dream up.

DAIRY-FREE, VEGAN

PREP TIME: 5 minutes
COOK TIME: 35 minutes

VARIATION TIP: Add even more kick to your mole sauce by adding in a jalapeño, stemmed and cored (remove seeds and membrane), in step 2.

- 2 tablespoons extra-virgin olive oil
- 1 white onion, peeled and quartered
- 4 garlic cloves
- ¼ cup chili powder
- 2 tablespoons all-purpose flour
- 1 teaspoon ground cinnamon
- 1 teaspoon ground cumin
- ½ teaspoon dried oregano
- 2½ cups vegetable stock
- 2 tablespoons almond butter
- 1 tablespoon tomato paste
- 1 tablespoon unsweetened cocoa powder
- 1 teaspoon sea salt

1. Place the olive oil, onion, and garlic into the blender pitcher. Select SAUTÉ.

2. With 2 minutes remaining in the program, add the chili powder, flour, cinnamon, cumin, and oregano to the blender pitcher in the order listed.

3. After the SAUTÉ program is complete, add the vegetable stock, almond butter, tomato paste, cocoa powder, and salt and select SAUCE/DIP.

4. Let the sauce cool to room temperature, then refrigerate in an airtight container for up to 3 days.

Per serving (½ cup): Calories: 185; Total fat: 13g; Saturated fat: 2g; Cholesterol: 0mg; Sodium: 443mg; Carbohydrates: 17g; Fiber: 5g; Protein: 4g

Tzatziki Sauce

MAKES 3 CUPS

I can't take any credit for this recipe—it was all my husband. Julien feels about tzatziki the way I feel about pesto—it makes everything better. Cool and creamy tzatziki is the perfect complement to any spicy dish. However, it also has a zing from the garlic and the dill, so it holds up well on its own. Try serving it with fresh pita and veggie slices or use it as a complement or dressing for your favorite Mediterranean dish.

GLUTEN-FREE, NUT-FREE, VEGETARIAN, FAMILY FAVORITE

PREP TIME: 35 minutes
BLEND TIME: 1 minute

VARIATION TIP: Add some fresh mint before you blend for a slightly different flavor!

1 English cucumber, peeled and diced

1 tablespoon sea salt, plus more for seasoning

3 cups plain Greek yogurt

Juice of 2 lemons

2 garlic cloves

1 tablespoon fresh dill

Freshly ground black pepper, to taste

1. Place the diced cucumber in a colander and sprinkle with some of the sea salt. Cover with a heavy dish and let sit for 30 minutes. Drain and pat dry with a paper towel.

2. Place the cucumber, salt, Greek yogurt, lemon juice, garlic, dill, and pepper into the blender pitcher in the order listed.

3. Select BLEND, then choose HIGH. Blend for 1 minute, or until the desired consistency is reached.

4. Store in an airtight container and refrigerate for 3 or 4 days.

Per serving (½ cup): *Calories: 88; Total fat: 4g; Saturated fat: 3g; Cholesterol: 16mg; Sodium: 251mg; Carbohydrates: 9g; Fiber: 0g; Protein: 5g*

Basil Pesto

MAKES 1 CUP

We always have a batch of fresh, homemade pesto in the refrigerator, because it is incredibly versatile and can be used on everything from warm farro bowls to pasta or pizza, and even as a delicious dipping sauce. While basil pesto is traditionally made using a mortar and pestle, the Foodi™ Blender makes short work of pulling this sauce together with much less effort. Whip up a batch and follow my motto: when in doubt, add a dollop of pesto.

GLUTEN-FREE, VEGETARIAN, UNDER 30 MINUTES, FAMILY FAVORITE

PREP TIME: 5 minutes
BLEND TIME: 1 minute

1 cup fresh basil leaves

3 cloves garlic

¼ cup pine nuts

⅓ cup freshly grated Parmigiano-Reggiano cheese

Sea salt, to taste

Freshly ground black pepper, to taste

⅓ cup extra-virgin olive oil

1. Place the basil, garlic, pine nuts, cheese, salt, and pepper into the blender pitcher in the order listed.

2. PULSE 4 times, then remove the cap on the lid. Select BLEND and choose LOW. While the ingredients are blending, slowly pour the olive oil into the blender pitcher until the mixture is fully emulsified.

3. Store the pesto in an airtight container; it keeps in the refrigerator for up to 1 week.

Per serving (2 tablespoons): Calories: 128; Total fat: 13g; Saturated fat: 2g; Cholesterol: 4mg; Sodium: 64mg; Carbohydrates: 1g; Fiber: 0g; Protein: 2g

Marinara Sauce

MAKES 5 CUPS

While I know there is a time and a place for spending hours making traditional tomato sauce on the stove, sweating down mirepoix, *layering and building amazing flavors, I also know that sometimes you need a quick and simple marinara sauce that doesn't take half a day to make. Instead of reaching for something from a jar, try this recipe the next time you are in a pinch. I love using this Marinara Sauce on pizza, cauliflower gnocchi, and everything in between.*

DAIRY-FREE, GLUTEN-FREE, NUT-FREE, VEGAN, FAMILY FAVORITE

PREP TIME: 5 minutes
COOK TIME: 35 minutes

3 tablespoons olive oil, divided

1 yellow onion, peeled and quartered

2 cloves garlic, peeled

2 tablespoons tomato paste

3 (14.5-ounce) cans whole peeled tomatoes

2 tablespoons chopped fresh basil

1 teaspoon granulated sugar

1 teaspoon sea salt

¼ teaspoon dried oregano

¼ teaspoon freshly ground black pepper

1. Place 2 tablespoons olive oil, onion, garlic, and tomato paste into the blender pitcher in the order listed. Select SAUTÉ.

2. Add the whole peeled tomatoes, basil, sugar, salt, oregano, and pepper to the blender pitcher and select SAUCE/DIP.

3. Store in an airtight container and refrigerate for 3 or 4 days.

Per serving (½ cup): Calories: 68; Total fat: 4g; Saturated fat: 1g; Cholesterol: 0mg; Sodium: 294mg; Carbohydrates: 8g; Fiber: 3g; Protein: 1g

Spicy Arrabbiata Sauce

MAKES 5 CUPS

If you like heat, then you have to try this spicy pasta sauce. Arrabbiata literally means "angry" in Italian, which refers to the spiciness that the red pepper flakes bring to this classic spicy marinara. Toss with penne and sprinkle with a little Parmesan cheese—you'll be asking yourself how something so simple can be so delicious!

GLUTEN-FREE, NUT-FREE

PREP TIME: 5 minutes
COOK TIME: 35 minutes

2 tablespoons butter

1 yellow onion, peeled and quartered

4 cloves garlic, peeled

2 teaspoons red pepper flakes

3 (14.5-ounce) cans whole peeled tomatoes

½ cup fresh basil

1 teaspoon sea salt

½ teaspoon freshly ground black pepper

1. Place the butter, onion, garlic, and red pepper flakes into the blender pitcher in the order listed. Select SAUTÉ.

2. Add the whole peeled tomatoes, basil, salt, and pepper, and select SAUCE/DIP.

3. Store in an airtight container and refrigerate for 3 or 4 days.

Per serving (½ cup): *Calories: 45; Total fat: 2g; Saturated fat: 1g; Cholesterol: 6mg; Sodium: 291mg; Carbohydrates: 6g; Fiber: 1g; Protein: 1g*

Puttanesca Sauce

Recipes for puttanesca sauce differ according to preference, and this version is based on the recipe from Naples, which is prepared without anchovies. (That said, if you prefer to add anchovies, simply do so in step 1.) I love the way the briny olives and capers meld with the acidity of the tomatoes to build a rich, robust flavor. Whip up this simple sauce and serve tossed with your favorite spaghetti for a traditional "alla puttanesca" meal.

DAIRY-FREE, GLUTEN-FREE, NUT-FREE, VEGAN

PREP TIME: 5 minutes
COOK TIME: 35 minutes

- 3 tablespoons olive oil, divided
- 1 yellow onion, peeled and quartered
- 2 cloves garlic, peeled
- ¼ teaspoon red pepper flakes
- 2 tablespoons tomato paste
- 3 (14.5-ounce) cans whole peeled tomatoes
- 2 tablespoons chopped fresh parsley
- 3 tablespoons chopped kalamata olives
- 2 tablespoons capers
- ¼ teaspoon sea salt
- ¼ teaspoon freshly ground black pepper

1. Place 2 tablespoons olive oil, onion, garlic, red pepper flakes, and tomato paste into the blender pitcher in the order listed. Select SAUTÉ.

2. Add remaining ingredients, and select SAUCE/DIP.

3. Store in an airtight container and refrigerate for 3 or 4 days.

Per serving: Calories: 71; Total fat: 5g; Saturated fat: 1g; Cholesterol: 0mg; Sodium: 482mg; Carbohydrates: 7g; Fiber: 2g; Protein: 1g

Creamy Garlic Alfredo Sauce

MAKES 5 CUPS

This Creamy Garlic Alfredo Sauce is velvety smooth and packed full of garlicky goodness. Toss some of this cheesy sauce with your favorite pasta, slather it on pizza, or spoon it over roasted chicken. Alfredo sauce is a great alternative to red sauce in just about any recipe.

GLUTEN-FREE, NUT-FREE, VEGETARIAN, 5-INGREDIENT

PREP TIME: 5 minutes
COOK TIME: 35 minutes

VARIATION TIP: Put your own twist on this creamy alfredo sauce—try adding roasted red peppers, buffalo sauce, pesto, bacon, or smoked sausage!

2 tablespoons butter

4 garlic cloves

16 ounces heavy cream

8 ounces cream cheese, quartered

2 cups grated Parmesan cheese

1. Place the butter and garlic into the blender pitcher. Select SAUTÉ.

2. Add the heavy cream, cream cheese, and Parmesan into the blender pitcher and select SAUCE/DIP.

3. Store in an airtight container and refrigerate for 3 or 4 days.

Per serving (½ cup): *Calories: 349; Total fat: 33g; Saturated fat: 20g; Cholesterol: 113mg; Sodium: 396mg; Carbohydrates: 3g; Fiber: 0g; Protein: 10g*

Pink Lemonade,
page 122

7

Infused Waters, Tonics, and Mixers

Pink Lemonade

SERVES 4

Bright, tart, and lightly sweet lemonade is the quintessential summer drink. Chances are, if you make lemonade at home, you are using a concentrate filled with sugar, because it is a quick and easy solution. However, with the Foodi™ Blender you can make a simple, 4-ingredient lemonade in about 15 minutes, start to finish! In this version, strawberries lend a bright pink hue and a sweet contrast to the tart flavor in this refreshing drink!

DAIRY-FREE, GLUTEN-FREE, NUT-FREE, VEGAN, UNDER 30 MINUTES, FAMILY FAVORITE, 5-INGREDIENT

PREP TIME: 5 minutes
COOK TIME: 10 minutes

VARIATION TIP: Make traditional lemonade by omitting the strawberry from this recipe, or make your own flavor combination by swapping the strawberries with blueberries, blackberries, mangos, etc.

½ cup granulated sugar

1 large lemon, quartered, plus more for garnish

1 cup strawberries

4 cups water

1. Place the sugar, lemon, strawberries, and water into the blender pitcher. Select WATER.

2. Pour the mixture through a strainer and discard the pulp.

3. Pour the lemonade over ice and garnish with fresh lemon slices.

Per serving: *Calories: 114; Total fat: 0g; Saturated fat: 0g; Cholesterol: 0mg; Sodium: 1mg; Carbohydrates: 31g; Fiber: 2g; Protein: 1g*

Lemon-Ginger Simple Syrup

MAKES 1 CUP

We always keep a bottle of this Lemon-Ginger Simple Syrup in the refrigerator, because it tastes great added to a variety of hot and cold drinks. Flavored with fresh ginger and lemon, you can swirl it into a mug of hot water in the morning, drizzle it into a glass of sparkling water for a homemade ginger ale, or enjoy it in the evening with a splash of rum.

DAIRY-FREE,
GLUTEN-FREE, NUT-FREE,
VEGAN, UNDER 30
MINUTES, 5-INGREDIENT

PREP TIME: 5 minutes
COOK TIME: 10 minutes

1 lemon, quartered

1 (2-inch) piece ginger,
  cut in thin slices

1 teaspoon ground turmeric

1 cup granulated sugar

1 cup water

1. Place the lemon, ginger, turmeric, sugar, and water into the blender pitcher in the order listed. Select MIXER.

2. Pour the mixture through a strainer and discard the pulp.

3. Store in an airtight container. The syrup will keep for up to a week in the refrigerator.

Per serving (2 tablespoons): Calories: 100; Total fat: 0g; Saturated fat: 0g; Cholesterol: 0mg; Sodium: 0mg; Carbohydrates: 27g; Fiber: 1g; Protein: 0g

Lemonade Peach Tea

SERVES 4

On hot summer days, an iced tea-lemonade is my favorite afternoon pick-me-up. This recipe was inspired by my favorite tea at Starbucks—I love that the black tea has a punch of caffeine, the tart lemonade adds the perfect amount of sweetness, and the peach balances everything out. The perfect drink for an afternoon refreshment!

DAIRY-FREE,
GLUTEN-FREE,
NUT-FREE, VEGAN,
UNDER 30 MINUTES,
FAMILY FAVORITE

PREP TIME: 5 minutes
COOK TIME: 10 minutes

VARIATION TIP: Put your own spin on this recipe by swapping the black tea with herbal or green tea, if you prefer. You can also swap the peaches for whatever fruit you have on hand!

½ cup granulated sugar

1 large lemon, quartered

1 cup peaches, cut into 1½-inch pieces

3 black tea bags, tea removed, bags discarded

4 cups water

Fresh mint, for garnish

1. Place the sugar, lemon, peaches, loose black tea, and water into the blender pitcher in the order listed. Select WATER.

2. Pour the mixture through a strainer and discard the pulp.

3. Pour the lemonade over ice and garnish with fresh mint.

Per serving: Calories: 117; Total fat: 0g; Saturated fat: 0g; Cholesterol: 0mg; Sodium: 1mg; Carbohydrates: 32g; Fiber: 2g; Protein: 1g

Raspberry-Lime Infused Water

SERVES 4

There are so many flavored water options these days, from fizzy to flat, fruity to floral, and everything in between. We always have a few ready-made options in the refrigerator to take on the go, but I love creating my own infused water from fresh fruits and herbs as a refreshing drink! My husband Julien's favorite flavor combo is Raspberry-Lime, so this recipe is in heavy rotation at our house.

DAIRY-FREE,
GLUTEN-FREE, NUT-FREE,
VEGETARIAN, FAMILY
FAVORITE, 5-INGREDIENT

PREP TIME: 5 minutes
COOK TIME: 10 minutes
CHILL TIME: 2 hours

SERVING TIP: For best results and the strongest flavor, I recommend chilling infused water for at least 1 hour before serving. You can also serve immediately over ice, but the flavor may dilute just a bit.

4 cups water

1 lime, quartered

1 cup raspberries, plus more for garnish

2 tablespoons honey (optional)

Fresh mint, for garnish

1. Place the water, lime, raspberries, and honey (if using) into the blender pitcher. Select WATER.

2. Pour the mixture through a strainer and discard the pulp.

3. Chill for at least 2 hours in the refrigerator before serving.

4. Serve the Raspberry-Lime Infused Water over ice and garnish with fresh mint.

Per serving: Calories: 21; Total fat: 0g; Saturated fat: 0g; Cholesterol: 0mg; Sodium: 1mg; Carbohydrates: 5g; Fiber: 2g; Protein: 0g

Mint and Berry Refresher

SERVES 4

The Foodi™ Blender makes it easy to infuse water with your favorite flavors and ingredients. Not only are infused waters a great way to stay hydrated, but they are also a fun way to elevate your refreshment table the next time you are entertaining. This Mint and Berry Refresher is one of my favorite recipes to make when I have friends over, because it is thirst-quenching, full of flavor, and pairs well with a splash of vodka. Not to mention it is beautiful, thanks to a handful of fresh fruit and a bit of the berry pulp.

DAIRY-FREE,
GLUTEN-FREE,
NUT-FREE, VEGETARIAN

PREP TIME: 5 minutes
COOK TIME: 10 minutes
CHILL TIME: 2 hours

VARIATION TIP: While most people prefer to discard the pulp from the fruit from infused water recipes, I like to add a little bit for a festive touch. Simply skip the straining step or reserve the pulp for garnish.

4 cups water

1 lime, quartered

1 cup blueberries, plus more for garnish

1 cup blackberries, plus more for garnish

2 teaspoons fresh basil, plus more for garnish

2 tablespoons honey (optional)

Fresh fruit, for garnish

Fresh mint, for garnish

1. Place the water, lime, blueberries, blackberries, basil, and honey (if using) into the blender pitcher in the order listed. Select WATER.

2. Pour the mixture through a strainer and discard the pulp.

3. Chill for at least 2 hours in the refrigerator before serving.

4. Serve the Mint and Berry Refresher over ice and garnish with fresh fruit and mint.

Per serving: Calories: 42; Total fat: 0g; Saturated fat: 0g; Cholesterol: 0mg; Sodium: 1mg; Carbohydrates: 11g; Fiber: 3g; Protein: 1g

Prickly Pear Tonic

SERVES 4

Herbal tonics have long been touted for their medicinal properties. Similar to tea, herbal tonics are made by infusing fruits and herbs into water. Tonics can be used as a remedy for a variety of ailments depending on the herbs used. This recipe for Prickly Pear Tonic has a variety of fruits and citrus for flavor along with ginger and turmeric—spices known for their anti-inflammatory properties. This tonic is delicious served hot or over ice!

DAIRY-FREE,
GLUTEN-FREE, NUT-FREE,
VEGETARIAN, UNDER
30 MINUTES

PREP TIME: 5 minutes
COOK TIME: 10 minutes

5 cups water

2 prickly pears, sliced

1 grapefruit, peeled
  and quartered

1 lemon, quartered

1 cup fresh mint

1 (2-inch) piece ginger,
  cut in thin slices

1 teaspoon ground turmeric

2 tablespoons honey

1. Place the water, prickly pear, grapefruit, lemon, mint, ginger, turmeric, and honey into the blender pitcher in the order listed. Select WATER.

2. Pour the mixture through a strainer and discard the pulp.

3. Pour the Prickly Pear Tonic over ice or serve hot, as desired.

Per serving: *Calories: 81; Total fat: 0g; Saturated fat: 0g; Cholesterol: 0mg; Sodium: 6mg; Carbohydrates: 22g; Fiber: 4g; Protein: 1g*

Vanilla-Cherry Mixer

MAKES 1 CUP

This recipe for Vanilla-Cherry Mixer is based on a popular flavor combination that is used for a variety of sugary sodas, but this version is made from healthy whole ingredients. Use it as a mix-in for homemade sodas, cocktails, and mocktails. Add more or less mixer based on how strong you want the flavor or add a splash of bourbon or rum for a cocktail spritzer, and most of all, enjoy!

DAIRY-FREE,
GLUTEN-FREE, NUT-FREE,
VEGAN, UNDER 30
MINUTES, 5-INGREDIENT

PREP TIME: 5 minutes
COOK TIME: 10 minutes

DID YOU KNOW? Homemade mixers are very concentrated, so they will last for a while. Make a batch in advance, store in an airtight container, and refrigerate for up to a week.

2 teaspoons vanilla extract
2 cups fresh cherries, pitted
½ cup maple syrup
1 cup water

1. Place the vanilla extract, cherries, maple syrup, and water into the blender pitcher in the order listed. Select MIXER.

2. Pour the mixture through a strainer and discard the pulp.

Per serving (2 tablespoons): Calories: 77; Total fat: 0g; Saturated fat: 0g; Cholesterol: 0mg; Sodium: 2mg; Carbohydrates: 19g; Fiber: 1g; Protein: 0g

Grapefruit-Basil Mixer

MAKES 1 CUP

Craft cocktails and mocktails are a fun and festive addition to any get-together. Plus, one batch of mixer is enough to supply an entire party! Whip up this Grapefruit-Basil Mixer and you are sure to impress your guests. Make a few different mixers and you can display them for a DIY refreshment bar. Poured into a nice glass bottle, this mixer also makes a great host(ess) gift!

DAIRY-FREE, GLUTEN-FREE, NUT-FREE, VEGETARIAN, UNDER 30 MINUTES, 5-INGREDIENT

PREP TIME: 5 minutes
COOK TIME: 10 minutes

VARIATION TIP: Homemade mixers are easy to make on your own; swap the fruit for what is in season or on hand—try raspberries, blueberries, blackberries, peaches, nectarines, and rhubarb. You can also use different herbs and spices. Follow the recommendations in the chart on page 27. The possibilities are endless!

2 teaspoons fresh basil

2 cups fresh grapefruit, peeled and quartered

½ cup honey

1 cup water

1. Place the basil, grapefruit, honey, and water into the blender pitcher into the order listed. Select MIXER.

2. Pour the mixture through a strainer and discard the pulp.

3. Store in an airtight container. The mixer will keep for up to a week in the refrigerator.

Per serving (2 tablespoons): Calories: 82; Total fat: 0g; Saturated fat: 0g; Cholesterol: 0mg; Sodium: 1mg; Carbohydrates: 22g; Fiber: 1g; Protein: 0g

Strawberry-Lime Mixer

MAKES 1 CUP

Flavored mixers can be used to elevate any homemade drink or cocktail. Try a splash in a glass of champagne (for the adults) or mixed in soda water for a refreshing summer soda (for the kids). This sweet strawberry mixer has a zing of lime and radiates summertime, but it can be used for so many things beyond drinks! Enjoy it drizzled over ice cream, pancakes, or even cheesecake!

DAIRY-FREE, GLUTEN-FREE, NUT-FREE, VEGAN, UNDER 30 MINUTES, 5-INGREDIENT

PREP TIME: 5 minutes
COOK TIME: 10 minutes

SUBSTITUTION TIP:
I recommend using fresh fruit and berries for mixers based on what is in season, but if you don't have any fresh fruit on hand, swap in 2 cups of frozen fruit or berries.

3 tablespoons fresh lime juice

2 cups fresh strawberries, halved

½ cup granulated sugar

1 cup water

1. Place the lime juice, strawberries, sugar, and water into the blender pitcher in the order listed. Select MIXER.

2. Pour the mixture through a strainer and discard the pulp.

3. Store in an airtight container. The mixer will keep for up to a week in the refrigerator.

Per serving (2 tablespoons): Calories: 62; Total fat: 0g; Saturated fat: 0g; Cholesterol: 0mg; Sodium: 1mg; Carbohydrates: 16g; Fiber: 1g; Protein: 0g

Fresh Mint Simple Syrup

MAKES 1 CUP

Simple syrup is an essential ingredient in a variety of cocktails and other beverages because it blends so well with other liquids. While it may sound intimidating, the truth is that, just as the name implies, it's relatively simple to make. Merely combine equal parts sugar and water and choose the MIXER program! You can even add your favorite flavorings, like mint or vanilla. This Fresh Mint Simple Syrup is perfect for sweetening your morning cup of coffee or tea, drizzling on a warm cake as a glaze, or as a delicious addition to a fresh fruit dessert like Mango Sorbet (page 189).

DAIRY-FREE, GLUTEN-FREE, NUT-FREE, VEGAN, UNDER 30 MINUTES, 5-INGREDIENT

PREP TIME: 5 minutes
COOK TIME: 10 minutes

1½ cups fresh mint leaves, roughly chopped

1 cup granulated sugar

1 cup water

1. Place the mint, sugar, and water into the blender pitcher in the order listed. Select MIXER.

2. Pour the mixture through a strainer and discard the pulp.

3. Store in an airtight container. The syrup will keep for up to a week in the refrigerator.

Per serving (2 tablespoons): Calories: 100; Total fat: 0g; Saturated fat: 0g; Cholesterol: 0mg; Sodium: 1mg; Carbohydrates: 26g; Fiber: 0g; Protein: 0g

Pineapple Margarita, *page 138*

8

Frozen Drinks

Pineapple Margarita

SERVES 4

A classic frozen drink, the margarita can take on many forms based on the flavors you like to add into it! My personal favorite is this sweet and tangy tropical version made with pineapple. The beauty of this recipe is how easy it is to change up—try strawberry, mango, or combining two kinds of fruit!

DAIRY-FREE, GLUTEN-FREE, NUT-FREE, VEGAN, UNDER 30 MINUTES, 5-INGREDIENT

PREP TIME: 5 minutes
BLEND TIME: 1 minute

VARIATION TIP: Simplify this easy recipe even further by replacing the lime juice and triple sec with ½ cup premade margarita mix.

4 cups frozen pineapple chunks

2 cups ice cubes

4 ounces tequila

4 ounces fresh lime juice

2 ounces triple sec

1. Place the pineapple, ice cubes, tequila, lime juice, and triple sec into the blender pitcher in the order listed.

2. Select FROZEN DRINK.

3. Pour into four glasses and enjoy.

Per serving: Calories: 210; Total fat: 0g; Saturated fat: 0g; Cholesterol: 0mg; Sodium: 0mg; Carbohydrates: 22g; Fiber: 0g; Protein: 1g

Frozen Raspberry Lemonade

SERVES 4

Sweet raspberries make a great partner for tart lemons in this frozen take on a classic American summertime drink. With the power of the Ninja® Foodi™ Blender's high-speed crushing blades, you'll be able to break down all of those raspberries for a smooth and refreshing frozen treat in no time.

DAIRY-FREE, GLUTEN-FREE, NUT-FREE, VEGAN, UNDER 30 MINUTES, FAMILY FAVORITE, 5-INGREDIENT

PREP TIME: 5 minutes
BLEND TIME: 1 minute

VARIATION TIP: Put your own spin on this recipe by swapping out the raspberries for any other berries you prefer!

6 cups ice cubes
1 cup raspberries
1 cup water
1 cup lemon juice
⅔ cup sugar

1. Place the ice cubes, raspberries, water, lemon juice, and sugar into the blender pitcher in the order listed.

2. Select FROZEN DRINK.

3. Pour into four glasses and enjoy.

Per serving: Calories: 159; Total fat: 0g; Saturated fat: 0g; Cholesterol: 0mg; Sodium: 1mg; Carbohydrates: 42g; Fiber: 2g; Protein: 1g

Frozen Sangria

SERVES 4

Take this summertime favorite to the next level by blending it with ice! The combination of refreshing fruit and red wine makes this a sweet frozen treat perfect for all of your adult guests at your next warm-weather get-together.

DAIRY-FREE, GLUTEN-FREE, NUT-FREE, VEGAN, UNDER 30 MINUTES

PREP TIME: 5 minutes
BLEND TIME: 1 minute

DID YOU KNOW?: You can use your favorite red wine to put your own unique spin on this recipe, but I recommend something light and fruity, like a pinot noir.

2 cups ice cubes

¾ cup frozen strawberries

½ cup frozen blueberries

16 ounces red wine

Juice of 1 orange

4 ounces triple sec

½ cup fresh raspberries

1 tablespoon sugar

Orange slices, for garnish (optional)

1. Place the ice cubes, strawberries, blueberries, red wine, orange juice, triple sec, raspberries, and sugar into the blender pitcher in the order listed.

2. Select FROZEN DRINK.

3. Pour into four glasses, garnish with orange slices, and enjoy.

Per serving: *Calories: 289; Total fat: 0g; Saturated fat: 0g; Cholesterol: 0mg; Sodium: 9mg; Carbohydrates: 16g; Fiber: 2g; Protein: 1g*

Bourbon-Peach Slush

Sweet peaches are a perfect pairing for spicy and smoky bourbon. While you may find them muddled with mint in a "smash" style cocktail, we're using frozen peaches here to make a cool, boozy treat. Add some mint leaves in before blending for an extra bit of freshness!

DAIRY-FREE, GLUTEN-FREE, NUT-FREE, VEGAN, UNDER 30 MINUTES

PREP TIME: 5 minutes
BLEND TIME: 1 minute

1 cup ice

3 cups frozen peaches

1 cup ginger ale

5 ounces bourbon

Juice of 1 lime

1 tablespoon sugar

1. Place the ice, peaches, ginger ale, bourbon, lime juice, and sugar into the blender pitcher in the order listed.

2. Select FROZEN DRINK.

3. Pour into four glasses and enjoy.

Per serving: Calories: 159; Total fat: 0g; Saturated fat: 0g; Cholesterol: 0mg; Sodium: 4mg; Carbohydrates: 20g; Fiber: 2g; Protein: 1g

Frozen Rum Punch

SERVES 4

Bring the taste of the tropics right into your kitchen with this citrusy and sweet rum punch. Serve this at your next party and let your guests garnish their own glasses with fun straws and fresh fruit, like pineapple chunks, orange slices, or strawberries!

DAIRY-FREE, GLUTEN-FREE, NUT-FREE, VEGAN, UNDER 30 MINUTES

PREP TIME: 5 minutes
BLEND TIME: 1 minute

1 (12-ounce) can frozen lemonade

1 cup ice cubes

16 ounces pineapple juice

8 ounces orange juice

10 ounces coconut rum

4 ounces lemon-lime soda

1. Place the frozen lemonade, ice cubes, pineapple juice, orange juice, coconut rum, and lemon-lime soda into the blender pitcher in the order listed.

2. Select FROZEN DRINK.

3. Pour into four glasses and enjoy.

Per serving: *Calories: 409; Total fat: 0g; Saturated fat: 0g; Cholesterol: 0mg; Sodium: 9mg; Carbohydrates: 63g; Fiber: 1g; Protein: 1g*

Frozen Negroni

SERVES 4

This popular cocktail can be found at almost any bar in Italy—and is gaining a lot of love here in the United States as well. While the original is stirred and strained over a chilled glass of ice, this version blends everything together into an Italian-inspired adult slush. Enjoy before dinner, like the classic is meant to be—or switch it up and have one whenever you'd like!

DAIRY-FREE, GLUTEN-FREE, NUT-FREE, VEGAN, UNDER 30 MINUTES, 5-INGREDIENT

PREP TIME: 5 minutes
BLEND TIME: 1 minute

VARIATION TIP: Turn this into an Americano, a "close relative" of the Negroni, by replacing the gin with seltzer or sparkling water.

3 cups ice cubes

8 ounces orange juice

2.5 ounces Campari

2.5 ounces gin

2.5 ounces vermouth

1. Place the ice cubes, orange juice, Campari, gin, and sweet vermouth into the blender pitcher in the order listed.

2. Select FROZEN DRINK.

3. Pour into four glasses and enjoy.

Per serving: *Calories: 130; Total fat: 0g; Saturated fat: 0g; Cholesterol: 0mg; Sodium: 1mg; Carbohydrates: 12g; Fiber: 0g; Protein: 0g*

Frozen Coconut Mojito

SERVES 4

There is a Cuban restaurant here in Boston that has an incredible food menu—but what makes it a true destination is the cocktail menu, complete with 53 varieties of mojitos! Inspired by their dedication to the drink, I've brought the flavors of a traditional mojito together with my favorite summertime cocktail—the piña colada—to create this Frozen Coconut Mojito.

DAIRY-FREE, GLUTEN-FREE, NUT-FREE, VEGAN, UNDER 30 MINUTES, 5-INGREDIENT

PREP TIME: 5 minutes
BLEND TIME: 1 minute

SUBSTITUTION TIP:
Don't have coconut rum on hand? Swap in an equal amount of white rum instead.

6 cups ice cubes

8 ounces coconut cream

8 ounces coconut rum

4 ounces lime juice

12 fresh mint leaves

1. Place the ice cubes, coconut cream, coconut rum, lime juice, and mint leaves into the blender pitcher in the order listed.

2. Select FROZEN DRINK.

3. Pour into four glasses and enjoy.

Per serving: *Calories: 320; Total fat: 19g; Saturated fat: 17g; Cholesterol: 0mg; Sodium: 3mg; Carbohydrates: 6g; Fiber: 1g; Protein: 2g*

Adult Minty Milkshake

SERVES 4

Ever since I was a little kid, I've loved the minty milkshakes that pop up at a certain fast-food restaurant for a limited time around St. Patrick's Day. My grandma used to take me every so often when they were on the menu. Here, I've recreated it in an adult version by using some vodka and bringing in the flavors of that childhood favorite with some minty liqueurs.

GLUTEN-FREE, NUT-FREE, VEGETARIAN, UNDER 30 MINUTES

PREP TIME: 5 minutes
BLEND TIME: 1 minute

2 cups vanilla ice cream

2.5 ounces vodka

2.5 ounces milk

2.5 ounces crème de menthe

1 ounce Irish crème liqueur

1 ounce peppermint schnapps

1. Place the ice cream, vodka, milk, crème de menthe, Irish crème liqueur, and peppermint schnapps into the blender pitcher in the order listed.

2. Select FROZEN DRINK.

3. Pour into four glasses and enjoy.

Per serving: Calories: 357; Total fat: 12g; Saturated fat: 7g; Cholesterol: 53mg; Sodium: 55mg; Carbohydrates: 33g; Fiber: 0g; Protein: 3g

Virgin Mango Piña Colada

SERVES 4

Piña colada literally translates to "strained pineapple." In this recipe, I'm keeping the flavors you know and love but adding in some sweet, juicy mango to really make it tropical—and skipping the rum, so you can enjoy this with family and friends of all ages.

DAIRY-FREE, GLUTEN-FREE, NUT-FREE, VEGAN, UNDER 30 MINUTES, FAMILY FAVORITE, 5-INGREDIENT

PREP TIME: 5 minutes
BLEND TIME: 1 minute

SUBSTITUTION TIP: If you can't find fresh pineapple that's perfectly ripe, swap in frozen pineapple chunks.

1 cup ice cubes

2 cups frozen mango chunks

⅔ cup coconut cream

Juice of 1 lime

1 cup fresh pineapple chunks

1. Place the ice cubes, mango, coconut cream, lime juice, and pineapple into the blender pitcher in the order listed.

2. Select FROZEN DRINK.

3. Pour into four glasses and enjoy.

Per serving: Calories: 206; Total fat: 14g; Saturated fat: 12g; Cholesterol: 0mg; Sodium: 4mg; Carbohydrates: 22g; Fiber: 2g; Protein: 2g

Watermelon-Lime Cooler

SERVES 4

This fruity drink is such a cinch to pull together—you'll be impressing your family and friends in no time! Because watermelon has such a high water content, there's no need to add any liquid besides the tart lime juice that gives this a tangy little bite.

DAIRY-FREE, GLUTEN-FREE, NUT-FREE, VEGAN, UNDER 30 MINUTES, 5-INGREDIENT

PREP TIME: 10 minutes
BLEND TIME: 1 minute

HACK IT: Cut and freeze your watermelon in advance and you can skip the ice cubes when making this recipe.

1 cup ice cubes

6 cups diced watermelon, seeded

Juice of 1 lime

1 tablespoon maple syrup

1. Place the ice cubes, watermelon, lime juice, and maple syrup into the blender pitcher in the order listed.

2. Select FROZEN DRINK.

3. Pour into four glasses and enjoy.

Per serving: Calories: 84; Total fat: 0g; Saturated fat: 0g; Cholesterol: 0mg; Sodium: 3mg; Carbohydrates: 21g; Fiber: 1g; Protein: 1g

Cinnamon-Infused
Whiskey, *page 158*

9

Infused Cocktails and Spirits

Pineapple-Infused Tequila

MAKES 4 CUPS

Infusing fruits and herbs into tequila is a simple and delicious way to add a bit of natural sweetness and flavor to your cocktails. Enjoy over ice or use as an ingredient in your favorite margarita recipe. If you want to add another punch of flavor, I recommend adding a jalapeño or sliced vanilla bean to the mix.

DAIRY-FREE,
GLUTEN-FREE,
NUT-FREE, VEGETARIAN,
VEGAN, 5-INGREDIENT

PREP TIME: 5 minutes
COOK TIME: 10 minutes
CHILL TIME: 2 hours

DID YOU KNOW? I find that silver tequila works best for infusing, but feel to use whatever you have on hand. You can also swap the tequila for vodka or another hard spirit.

32 ounces silver tequila　　**2 cups pineapple chunks**

1. Place the tequila and pineapple into the blender pitcher. Select COCKTAIL.

2. Pour the mixture through a strainer into an airtight jar. Discard the pulp.

3. Chill for at least 2 hours in the refrigerator before serving.

Per serving (2 ounces): Calories: 104; Total fat: 0g; Saturated fat: 0g; Cholesterol: 0mg; Sodium: 0mg; Carbohydrates: 2g; Fiber: 0g; Protein: 0g

Lavender-Rosemary Infused Vodka

Botanical cocktails are all the rage in restaurants and bars in my city this summer. The minty and peppery notes from the rosemary pair perfectly with herby lavender. Turn this into a fun concoction by adding some soda water, grapefruit juice, and lemon juice!

GLUTEN-FREE, DAIRY-FREE, NUT-FREE, VEGAN, 5-INGREDIENT

PREP TIME: 5 minutes
COOK TIME: 10 minutes
CHILL TIME: 2 hours

DID YOU KNOW? Fresh is best. When infusing spirits, always opt for fresh herbs over dried.

32 ounces vodka

1 sprig fresh rosemary, stemmed

2 sprigs fresh food-grade lavender, stemmed

1. Place the vodka, rosemary, and lavender into the blender pitcher. Select COCKTAIL.

2. Pour the mixture through a strainer into an airtight jar. Discard the pulp.

3. Chill for at least 2 hours in the refrigerator before serving.

Per serving (1 ounce): *Calories: 64; Total fat: 0g; Saturated fat: 0g; Cholesterol: 0mg; Sodium: 0mg; Carbohydrates: 0g; Fiber: 0g; Protein: 0g*

Cucumber and Lime Infused Gin

MAKES 5 CUPS

The combination of cooling cucumber and tangy lime pair perfectly in this simple yet flavorful infused gin recipe. Put a fresh twist on any gin-based cocktail, from a gin fizz to a gin gimlet. My husband Julien likes to step up his go-to gin and tonic with this recipe for a refreshing tart cocktail.

DAIRY-FREE,
GLUTEN-FREE, NUT-FREE,
VEGAN, 5-INGREDIENT

PREP TIME: 5 minutes
COOK TIME: 10 minutes
CHILL TIME: 2 hours

DID YOU KNOW?: The perfect gin and tonic is served over ice with a garnish of fresh mint and a lime wedge. Serve the gin and tonic anywhere between a 1:1 to 1:3 ratio, depending on your preference.

32 ounces gin

½ cucumber, roughly chopped

1 lime, quartered

1. Place the gin, cucumber, and lime into the blender pitcher in the order listed. Select COCKTAIL.

2. Pour the mixture through a strainer into an airtight jar. Discard the pulp.

3. Chill for at least 2 hours in the refrigerator before serving.

Per serving (1 ounce): *Calories: 52; Total fat: 0g; Saturated fat: 0g; Cholesterol: 0mg; Sodium: 0mg; Carbohydrates: 0g; Fiber: 0g; Protein: 0g*

Vanilla Bean and Orange Infused Bourbon

MAKES 4½ CUPS

This bourbon gets some sweet and citrusy additions when you infuse it with pieces of orange and whole vanilla beans. It gives you a great way to change up a classic old-fashioned and also tastes great in eggnog during the holiday season. You can also keep it simple and enjoy it neat!

GLUTEN-FREE, DAIRY-FREE, NUT-FREE, VEGAN, 5-INGREDIENT

PREP TIME: 5 minutes
COOK TIME: 10 minutes
CHILL TIME: 2 hours

SUBSTITUTION TIP: If you can't find vanilla beans, substitute with 2 tablespoons vanilla extract.

32 ounces bourbon
1 orange, quartered

2 vanilla beans, sliced down the middle

1. Place the bourbon, orange, and vanilla beans into the blender pitcher. Select COCKTAIL.

2. Pour the mixture through a strainer into an airtight jar. Discard the pulp.

3. Chill for at least 2 hours in the refrigerator before serving.

Per serving: Calories: 59; Total fat: 0g; Saturated fat: 0g; Cholesterol: 0mg; Sodium: 0mg; Carbohydrates: 0g; Fiber: 0g; Protein: 0g

Cinnamon-Infused Whiskey

MAKES 4 CUPS

Everywhere you look these days you can find that popular brand of cinnamon whiskey. Why not try your hand at a homemade version? This Cinnamon-Infused Whiskey is lightly sweetened and infused with whole cinnamon sticks. Add a spicy kick to this aromatic infusion by adding 3 or 4 dried red chile peppers to the blender in step 1.

GLUTEN-FREE,
DAIRY-FREE, NUT-FREE,
VEGAN, 5-INGREDIENT

PREP TIME: 5 minutes
COOK TIME: 10 minutes
CHILL TIME: 2 hours

DID YOU KNOW?: When choosing an alcohol to infuse, like whiskey, there's no need to go all out and buy a top-shelf bottle. Pick a cheap bottle and infuse it with spices and herbs.

32 ounces whiskey

6 to 8 cinnamon sticks

2 tablespoons granulated sugar (optional)

1. Place the whiskey, cinnamon sticks, and sugar (if using) into the blender pitcher. Select COCKTAIL.

2. Pour the mixture through a strainer into an airtight jar. Discard the pulp.

3. Chill for at least 2 hours in the refrigerator before serving.

Per serving (1 ounce): *Calories: 64; Total fat: 0g; Saturated fat: 0g; Cholesterol: 0mg; Sodium: 0mg; Carbohydrates: 0g; Fiber: 0g; Protein: 0g*

Spiced Hot Cider

SERVES 4

There's nothing like warm apple cider on a cold winter's night—except maybe this Spiced Hot Cider with a splash of rum! With the Foodi™ Blender, it couldn't be easier to whip up a comforting pitcher of cider that will fill your home with the aroma of cinnamon, apples, and fresh citrus. Enjoy a mug of cider by the fire or pour it in a thermos for a day of sledding and skating. If you are sharing with the kids, don't forget to omit the rum.

DAIRY-FREE, GLUTEN-FREE, NUT-FREE, VEGAN, UNDER 30 MINUTES

PREP TIME: 5 minutes
COOK TIME: 15 minutes

1 cinnamon stick, broken in half
32 ounces apple cider
8 ounces dark rum
1 navel orange, quartered
1 lemon, quartered
1 (1-inch) piece ginger, peeled and quartered
¼ cup brown sugar
1 teaspoon allspice

1. Place the cinnamon stick into the blender pitcher. Select SAUTÉ.

2. Add the apple cider, rum, orange, lemon, ginger, brown sugar, and allspice to the blender pitcher in the order listed. Select COCKTAIL.

3. Pour the mixture through a strainer into four mugs. Discard the pulp.

4. Serve warm and enjoy.

Per serving: *Calories: 306; Total fat: 0g; Saturated fat: 0g; Cholesterol: 0mg; Sodium: 15mg; Carbohydrates: 46g; Fiber: 2g; Protein: 1g*

Habanero-Infused Vodka

MAKES 4 CUPS

This vodka is not for the faint of heart—the Ninja® Foodi™ Blender is your partner in flavor infusion, meaning you'll get quite a kick from the habanero! Add this vodka to a batch of Bloody Mary cocktails at your next brunch and impress your guests with this spicy spirit that's full of heat, but simple to make.

GLUTEN-FREE, DAIRY-FREE, NUT-FREE, VEGAN, 5-INGREDIENT

PREP TIME: 5 minutes
COOK TIME: 10 minutes
CHILL TIME: 2 hours

SUBSTITUTION TIP: All of the infused spirits throughout this chapter can be made gluten-free by opting for a grain- and gluten-free alcohol, such as gluten-free vodka. This depends on the brand, so be sure to read the labels.

32 ounces vodka　　**1 habanero pepper**

1. Place the vodka and habanero pepper into the blender pitcher. Select COCKTAIL.

2. Pour the mixture through a strainer into an airtight jar. Discard the pulp.

3. Chill for at least 2 hours in the refrigerator before serving.

Per serving (1 ounce): *Calories: 65; Total fat: 0g; Saturated fat: 0g; Cholesterol: 0mg; Sodium: 0mg; Carbohydrates: 0g; Fiber: 0g; Protein: 0g*

Cape Cod Mule

SERVES 4

You might be asking yourself—what makes a mule a "Cape Cod Mule"? The Ninja® Test Kitchen is located just outside of Boston, less than an hour from a big area full of cranberry bogs right near Cape Cod! Infusing the vodka with cranberries in the Foodi™ Blender puts a tasty, tart spin on this popular cocktail. Serve it in a chilled copper mug over ice and enjoy!

GLUTEN-FREE, DAIRY-FREE, NUT-FREE, VEGAN, 5-INGREDIENT

PREP TIME: 5 minutes
COOK TIME: 10 minutes
CHILL TIME: 2 hours

DID YOU KNOW?
Because heating spirits can degrade the alcohol content, make sure to select the COCKTAIL button, which was specifically designed to work with spirits and cocktails.

32 ounces vodka
1 cup cranberries
4 limes, quartered

16 ounces ginger beer, for serving
Lime wedges, for garnish

1. Place the vodka, cranberries, and limes into the blender pitcher in the order listed. Select COCKTAIL.

2. Pour the mixture through a strainer into an airtight jar. Discard the pulp.

3. Chill for at least 2 hours in the refrigerator before serving.

4. Serve 2 ounces of the cranberry-lime infused vodka and 4 ounces of ginger beer over ice and garnish with a lime wedge.

Per serving: Calories: 582; Total fat: 0g; Saturated fat: 0g; Cholesterol: 0mg; Sodium: 15mg; Carbohydrates: 20g; Fiber: 3g; Protein: 1g

Lime and Jalapeño Margarita

MAKES 4½ CUPS

This spicy spin on a margarita is the perfect drink pairing for your next Taco Tuesday. Simply add all of the ingredients in the Foodi™ Blender and let it work its magic! Turn this into a frosty frozen margarita by adding the chilled drink back into the blender with some ice and selecting FROZEN DRINK.

DAIRY-FREE, GLUTEN-FREE, NUT-FREE, VEGAN

PREP TIME: 5 minutes
COOK TIME: 10 minutes
CHILL TIME: 2 hours

24 ounces tequila

8 ounces triple sec

4 limes, quartered

1 jalapeño, halved and seeded (if desired)

4 ounces agave syrup

Coarse sea salt, for garnish

Lime wedges, for garnish

1. Place the tequila, triple sec, limes, jalapeño, and agave syrup into the blender pitcher in the order listed. Select COCKTAIL.

2. Pour the mixture through a strainer into an airtight jar. Discard the pulp.

3. Chill for at least 2 hours in the refrigerator before serving.

4. Salt the rim of each glass and serve over ice, garnished with a lime wedge.

Per serving (4 ounces): Calories: 347; Total fat: 0g; Saturated fat: 0g; Cholesterol: 0mg; Sodium: 1mg; Carbohydrates: 25g; Fiber: 1g; Protein: 0g

Summertime Sangria

SERVES 6

Light, refreshing, and full of fruity flavors, this sangria is the only cocktail you'll want to drink all summer long. In fact, it is my go-to recipe whether we are hosting a summer cookout or celebrating the Fourth of July at a friend's house. Unlike classic sangria made with dark Spanish wine and orange juice, this rosé-based sangria is lighter, with a tangy-sweet finish. This recipe also uses fresh summer fruits so that every sip tastes like a ray of sunshine.

GLUTEN-FREE, DAIRY-FREE, NUT-FREE, VEGAN, UNDER 30 MINUTES, FAMILY FAVORITE

PREP TIME: 5 minutes
COOK TIME: 10 minutes

VARIATION TIP: Serve with a splash of sparkling water to turn this fruity cocktail into a Summertime Sangria Spritzer!

1 (750ml) bottle rosé wine
¼ cup brandy
1 lemon, cut into quarters
1 cup peach slices

1 cup raspberries
1 cup strawberries, halved
¼ cup granulated sugar

1. Place the rosé, brandy, lemon, peaches, raspberries, strawberries, and sugar into the blender pitcher in the order listed. Select COCKTAIL.

2. Pour the mixture through a strainer into an airtight jar. Discard the pulp.

3. Serve over ice and garnish with fresh fruit.

Per serving: Calories: 195; Total fat: 0g; Saturated fat: 0g; Cholesterol: 0mg; Sodium: 1mg; Carbohydrates: 17g; Fiber: 3g; Protein: 1g

Key Lime Pie,
page 170

10
Desserts

Key Lime Pie

Some of my favorite recipes throughout this book that I make frequently at home are what some might call semi-homemade—meaning the key ingredients are premade but are given a homemade feel with a few simple steps. For example, this recipe for Key Lime Pie uses a store-bought graham cracker crust, but the filling is made from scratch. Use this no-bake recipe for a simple summer dessert without turning on the oven!

NUT-FREE, VEGETARIAN

PREP TIME: 10 minutes
BLEND TIME: 1 minute
CHILL TIME: 3 or 4 hours

VARIATION TIP: Top your Key Lime Pie with a dollop of homemade Vanilla Whipped Cream (page 176).

1 (14-ounce) can sweetened condensed milk

1 (8-ounce) package of cream cheese, softened

½ cup fresh lime juice

1 tablespoon lime zest

1 teaspoon vanilla extract

1 premade graham cracker crust

1. Place condensed milk, cream cheese, lime juice and zest, and vanilla extract into the blender pitcher in the order listed.

2. Select BLEND then HIGH and run for 60 seconds. Scrape down the sides and repeat as needed until smooth.

3. Pour the pie filling into the graham cracker crust.

4. Place the pie in the refrigerator for 3 or 4 hours until it is well set.

Per serving: Calories: 373; Total fat: 20g; Saturated fat: 9g; Cholesterol: 47mg; Sodium: 248mg; Carbohydrates: 44g; Fiber: 0g; Protein: 7g

Pineapple Whip

This dairy-free pineapple sorbet is incredibly delicious and refreshing! Based on the soft-serve-style Dole Whip dessert that is making headlines at Disney, this version is made from just four simple ingredients and could not be easier to make. Be careful—this sweet treat is incredibly addicting!

DAIRY-FREE, GLUTEN-FREE, NUT-FREE, VEGAN, UNDER 30 MINUTES, 5-INGREDIENT

PREP TIME: 5 minutes
BLEND TIME: 1 minute

VARIATION TIP: Frozen treats and ice cream made in the Foodi™ Blender are a soft-serve consistency. If you prefer a traditional ice cream texture, place the ice cream in a loaf pan and freeze for at least 1 hour before serving.

4 cups frozen pineapple chunks

½ cup pineapple juice

½ cup canned coconut milk

1 tablespoon lemon juice

1. Place the pineapple chunks and juice, coconut milk, and lemon juice into the blender pitcher in the order listed.

2. Select ICE CREAM. Use the tamper to push the ingredients down toward the blades as needed during the program.

3. Stored in an airtight container, the ice cream keeps in the freezer for 5 days.

Per serving: *Calories: 146; Total fat: 6g; Saturated fat: 5g; Cholesterol: 0mg; Sodium: 6mg; Carbohydrates: 24g; Fiber: 0g; Protein: 2g*

Easy Lemon Curd

MAKES 1½ CUPS

Lemon curd is the basis of many of my favorite desserts—hello, lemon bars, lemon-mascarpone layer cake, and lemon meringue cheesecake! While you can find a premade version at many grocery stores, nothing compares to the flavor of this from-scratch lemon curd made with real lemons. In fact, when it is freshly made, you'll find me sneaking this Easy Lemon Curd onto just about any baked good. The best part is this deliciously tangy, creamy, and sweet curd comes together with just 5 simple ingredients.

GLUTEN-FREE, NUT-FREE, VEGETARIAN, 5-INGREDIENT

PREP TIME: 5 minutes
COOK TIME: 30 minutes
CHILL TIME: 1 hour

DID YOU KNOW? Keep this lemon curd fresh for up to a week by storing it in an airtight container and placing in the refrigerator.

3 large eggs
1 cup sugar
½ cup fresh-squeezed lemon juice

¼ cup unsalted butter
1 tablespoon lemon zest

1. Place the eggs, sugar, lemon juice, butter, and lemon zest into the blender pitcher in the order listed. Select SAUCE/DIP.

2. Pour into a heat-safe glass container and chill in the refrigerator at least 1 hour, or until it is well set, before serving.

Per serving (¼ cup): Calories: 237; Total fat: 10g; Saturated fat: 6g; Cholesterol: 126mg; Sodium: 36mg; Carbohydrates: 35g; Fiber: 0g; Protein: 3g

Creamy Vanilla Custard

SERVES 4

This no-bake Creamy Vanilla Custard is a gourmet version of vanilla pudding. It whips up into a frothy, sweet, and velvety treat that can be used as the base for a summer fruit tart, piled on top of pancakes, or served for dessert with cookies crumbled on top. If you are like me, you might even sneak a few bites before serving!

GLUTEN-FREE, NUT-FREE, VEGETARIAN, 5-INGREDIENT

PREP TIME: 5 minutes
COOK TIME: 10 minutes
BLEND TIME: 3 minutes

HACK IT: Rogue egg white strands can be removed from the custard by passing it through a fine-mesh sieve.

2 cups whole milk

2 tablespoons cornstarch

⅓ cup sugar

2 eggs, lightly beaten

1 teaspoon vanilla

1. Place the milk, cornstarch, and sugar into the blender pitcher in the order listed. Select SAUTÉ and allow to cook for 2 minutes.

2. Add the eggs and vanilla to the blender pitcher. Select SAUTÉ and allow to cook for 5 minutes.

3. Select BLEND then HIGH and run for about 30 seconds at a time, up to 3 minutes, until custard becomes thick and frothy. It may steam when you lift the lid.

4. Stored in an airtight container, this keeps in the refrigerator for 3 or 4 days.

Per serving: Calories: 191; Total fat: 6g; Saturated fat: 3g; Cholesterol: 118mg; Sodium: 84mg; Carbohydrates: 27g; Fiber: 0g; Protein: 7g

Tiramisu Mousse

SERVES 4

If there is tiramisu on the menu, you can bet that my husband, Julien, is ordering it for dessert. In honor of his favorite sweet treat, I developed this delicious, creamy mousse with all of the flavors of the traditional Italian dessert. Cream, cheese, chocolate, and coffee—what's not to love?

GLUTEN-FREE, NUT-FREE, VEGETARIAN, UNDER 30 MINUTES, FAMILY FAVORITE

PREP TIME: 5 minutes
BLEND TIME: 1 minute

SUBSTITUTION TIP: If mascarpone is not available, you can use cream cheese as a substitute.

1 cup heavy whipping cream
1½ cups powdered sugar
8 ounces mascarpone cheese
1 teaspoon vanilla extract
2 tablespoons brewed coffee, chilled
1 tablespoon unsweetened cocoa powder, plus more for serving

1. Place the heavy whipping cream into the blender pitcher.

2. Select BLEND then HIGH and run for 15 to 30 seconds, until the cream thickens.

3. Remove the whipped cream from the blender, transfer to a large mixing bowl, and place in the refrigerator.

4. Place the sugar, mascarpone cheese, vanilla extract, coffee, and cocoa powder into the blender pitcher in the order listed.

5. Select BLEND then HIGH and run for 15 to 30 seconds, until smooth.

6. Add the coffee mixture to the bowl of chilled whipped cream, and fold together. Place the Tiramisu Mousse into a large plastic bag, and snip off a small corner of the bag.

7. Pipe a small amount of the mousse into the bottom of 4 serving glasses. Top with a dusting of cocoa powder, and repeat.

Per serving: Calories: 629; Total fat: 48g; Saturated fat: 28g; Cholesterol: 0mg; Sodium: 152mg; Carbohydrates: 48g; Fiber: 1g; Protein: 6g

Vanilla Whipped Cream

MAKES 4 CUPS

Homemade whipped cream may sound intimidating, but it is truly one of the easiest recipes to make at home with a few simple ingredients. This Vanilla Whipped Cream elevates just about any dessert, from a berry trifle to cream puffs, and can be used to top everything from Key Lime Pie (page 170) to Minty Hot Chocolate (page 179).

GLUTEN-FREE, NUT-FREE, VEGETARIAN, UNDER 30 MINUTES, FAMILY FAVORITE, 5-INGREDIENT

PREP TIME: 5 minutes
BLEND TIME: 1 minute

VARIATION TIP: There are so many ways to switch up this recipe based on how you are serving the whipped cream! Swap out vanilla for maple syrup, cinnamon, almond extract, even chocolate chips!

2 cups heavy whipping cream
½ teaspoon vanilla extract
1 tablespoon sugar (optional)

1. Place the whipping cream, vanilla extract, and sugar into the blender pitcher in the order listed.

2. Select BLEND then HIGH and run for 15 to 30 seconds, until the cream thickens.

3. Stored in an airtight container, this keeps in the refrigerator for 2 or 3 days.

Per serving (¼ cup): Calories: 103; Total fat: 11g; Saturated fat: 7g; Cholesterol: 41mg; Sodium: 11mg; Carbohydrates: 1g; Fiber: 0g; Protein: 1g

Cannoli Dip

Cannoli are Italian pastries that originated on the island of Sicily and now are a staple of American Italian cuisine. When we visit the North End in Boston, I can't leave without stopping by my favorite pastry shop for a box of these delicious desserts. While I love the crispy fried dough that holds the pastry together, it is the sweet, creamy cheese filling that is my favorite part. This Cannoli Dip replicates that delicious creamy filling, so everyone can enjoy! Serve alongside cinnamon sugar pita chips or broken pieces of waffle cones.

GLUTEN-FREE, VEGETARIAN, UNDER 30 MINUTES

PREP TIME: 10 minutes
BLEND TIME: 1 minute

8 ounces mascarpone cheese

1½ cups whole-milk ricotta cheese

1¼ cups powdered sugar

¾ teaspoon vanilla extract

¾ teaspoon almond extract

¼ cup mini chocolate chips

1. Place the mascarpone cheese, ricotta cheese, sugar, vanilla extract, and almond extract into the blender pitcher in the order listed.

2. Select BLEND then HIGH and run for 60 seconds. Scrape down the sides and repeat as needed until smooth.

3. Pour the cheese mixture into a serving bowl, and top with the mini chocolate chips.

Per serving: *Calories: 294; Total fat: 21g; Saturated fat: 12g; Cholesterol: 59mg; Sodium: 55mg; Carbohydrates: 22g; Fiber: 0g; Protein: 7g*

Minty Hot Chocolate

SERVES 4

Ditch the powdered hot chocolate mix for this rich and creamy Minty Hot Chocolate recipe. I love making hot chocolate at home, but it can be difficult and messy to make on the stove, as you need to constantly watch the pot so it doesn't burn. I can't wait to blend up this recipe this winter and cuddle up on the couch with a mug of Minty Hot Chocolate and my favorite holiday movie!

GLUTEN-FREE, NUT-FREE, VEGETARIAN, UNDER 30 MINUTES, FAMILY FAVORITE

PREP TIME: 5 minutes
COOK TIME: 20 minutes

3 cups whole milk

1 cup half-and-half

1 cup milk chocolate chips

4 tablespoons mint chips

Mini marshmallows, for garnish

Chocolate syrup, for garnish

1. Place the milk, half-and-half, chocolate chips, and mint chips into the blender pitcher in the order listed.

2. Select TEMP MED and cook for 20 minutes. PULSE every 5 minutes to ensure even heating.

3. Pour into four mugs, garnish with marshmallows, and drizzle with chocolate syrup, as desired.

Per serving: Calories: 638; Total fat: 45g; Saturated fat: 26g; Cholesterol: 42mg; Sodium: 113mg; Carbohydrates: 47g; Fiber: 8g; Protein: 14g

Chocolate Fondue

SERVES 6 TO 8

Looking for a quick and easy dessert for a crowd? Try this Chocolate Fondue recipe for a quick and easy treat that is sure to bring everyone together. No need for a fancy chocolate fountain—simply combine the chocolate and heavy cream in the Foodi™ Blender and then serve the rich, chocolaty fondue in a heatproof glass bowl. Serve with fresh fruit, cookies, pretzels, pound cake, marshmallows, and anything else you can think of—just don't forget a big pile of toothpicks.

GLUTEN-FREE, NUT-FREE, VEGETARIAN, UNDER 30 MINUTES, 5-INGREDIENT

PREP TIME: 5 minutes
COOK TIME: 30 minutes

VARIATION TIP: Add ½ cup of smooth peanut butter to the pitcher with the chocolate chips to make this a Peanut Butter Cup Fondue!

1 (12-ounce) bag semisweet chocolate chips

1 cup heavy cream

Strawberries, for serving

Pineapple, cubed, for serving

Pound cake, cubed, for serving

1. Place the chocolate chips and heavy cream into the blender pitcher. Select SAUCE/DIP.

2. Serve the fondue warm with strawberries, pineapple cubes, and pound cake pieces for dipping.

Per serving: *Calories: 434; Total fat: 32g; Saturated fat: 19g; Cholesterol: 75mg; Sodium: 80mg; Carbohydrates: 33g; Fiber: 5g; Protein: 5g*

Chocolate Pudding Ice Cream

SERVES 4

Ridiculously rich and perfectly luscious, this pudding ice cream will delight true chocolate lovers. This decadent dessert is easy to make—it only requires two ingredients—but requires a little bit of planning for the best results. I recommend making the chocolate pudding cubes the night before (kudos if you keep a batch in the freezer for chocolate ice cream on the fly). Once your pudding cubes are frozen, pulling together this homemade ice cream only takes a few minutes!

GLUTEN-FREE, NUT-FREE, VEGETARIAN, 5-INGREDIENT

PREP TIME: 5 minutes
BLEND TIME: 1 minute
FREEZE TIME: 6+ hours

2½ cups plus 2 tablespoons whole milk, divided

1 (3.4-ounce) package chocolate instant pudding mix

1. In a large mixing bowl, whisk together 2 cups of whole milk and the chocolate pudding mix until combined.

2. Divide the mixture across two ice cube trays. Place the ice cube trays in the freezer and freeze for at least 6 hours.

3. Place the pudding cubes and the remaining milk into the blender pitcher.

4. Select ICE CREAM. Use the tamper to push the ingredients down toward the blades as needed during the program.

5. Stored in an airtight container, the ice cream keeps in the freezer for 5 days.

Per serving: Calories: 185; Total fat: 5g; Saturated fat: 3g; Cholesterol: 15mg; Sodium: 415mg; Carbohydrates: 30g; Fiber: 1g; Protein: 5g

Strawberry–Cream Cheese Ice Cream

SERVES 6 TO 8

Strawberry–Cream Cheese Ice Cream has long been a favorite of mine thanks to the combination of luscious cream cheese and sweet strawberries. It tastes like a frozen strawberry cheesecake. So when we replicated the recipe in the test kitchen a few years back, it quickly took over as a recipe we developed for just about every Ninja® blender. To amp up this Ninja Test Kitchen favorite, top it off with fresh strawberry compote from the Dutch Baby Pancake recipe (page 50).

GLUTEN-FREE, NUT-FREE, VEGETARIAN, UNDER 30 MINUTES, 5-INGREDIENT

PREP TIME: 5 minutes
BLEND TIME: 1 minute

VARIATION TIP: Frozen treats and ice cream made in the Foodi™ Blender are a soft-serve consistency. If you prefer a traditional ice cream texture, place the ice cream in a loaf pan and freeze for at least 1 hour before serving.

½ cup light cream
½ (8-ounce) package cream cheese, quartered
1 tablespoon fresh lemon juice
1 teaspoon vanilla extract
⅓ cup sugar
1½ cups frozen unsweetened strawberries
½ cup ice

1. Place the light cream, cream cheese, lemon juice, vanilla extract, sugar, frozen strawberries, and ice into the blender pitcher in the order listed.

2. Select ICE CREAM. Use the tamper to push the ingredients down toward the blades as needed during the program.

3. Stored in an airtight container, the ice cream keeps in the freezer for 5 days.

Per serving: *Calories: 145; Total fat: 9g; Saturated fat: 5g; Cholesterol: 28mg; Sodium: 69mg; Carbohydrates: 16g; Fiber: 1g; Protein: 2g*

Pots de Crème

SERVES 4

My personal philosophy is if it isn't chocolate, it isn't dessert. Luckily, these silky-smooth custard desserts are rich with chocolate. While this classic French dessert will taste like a labor of love, it is actually an easy, low-effort recipe. Wow your dinner party guests or indulge on date night at home. If you want to get fancy, top the finished ramekins with my Vanilla Whipped Cream (page 176) or drizzle with Fresh Mint Simple Syrup (page 135).

GLUTEN-FREE, NUT-FREE, VEGETARIAN, FAMILY FAVORITE

PREP TIME: 5 minutes
BLEND TIME: 3 minutes
COOK TIME: 30 minutes
CHILL TIME: 3 or 4 hours

- **8 ounces semisweet chocolate chips**
- **2 tablespoons sugar**
- **2 eggs, room temperature**
- **1 teaspoon vanilla extract**
- **Pinch sea salt**
- **½ cup plus 2 tablespoons heavy cream**

1. Place the chocolate chips, sugar, eggs, vanilla extract, salt, and heavy cream into the blender pitcher in the order listed. Select SAUCE/DIP.

2. Pour the mixture into 4 small cups or ramekins. Place the ramekins into the refrigerator and chill for 3 or 4 hours, until well set.

Per serving: Calories: 527; Total fat: 40g; Saturated fat: 23g; Cholesterol: 158mg; Sodium: 61mg; Carbohydrates: 33g; Fiber: 6g; Protein: 8g

Blueberry-Buttermilk Ice Cream

SERVES 6

Summer is all about consuming as much ice cream as humanly possible, and this Blueberry-Buttermilk Ice Cream tastes like summer. Packed with sweet blueberries, the buttermilk balances out the ice cream with a hint of tartness for the perfect balance. I promise you won't be able to eat just one scoop!

GLUTEN-FREE, NUT-FREE, VEGETARIAN

PREP TIME: 10 minutes
BLEND TIME: 1 minute
COOK TIME: 31 minutes
FREEZE TIME: 6+ hours

SUBSTITUTION TIP:
Frozen blueberries work equally well in this recipe.

2 cups buttermilk
1 cup evaporated milk
1 cup blueberries
⅓ cup granulated sugar
1 tablespoon lemon juice
¼ cup whole milk

1. In a medium bowl, stir together the buttermilk and evaporated milk. Pour into ice cube trays and freeze for at least 6 hours.

2. Place the blueberries, sugar, and lemon juice into the blender pitcher.

3. PULSE 3 times, then select SAUCE/DIP. Let contents cool for 5 minutes.

4. Place the frozen cream cubes and milk into the blender pitcher with the blueberry mixture.

5. Select ICE CREAM. Use the tamper to push the ingredients down toward the blades as needed during the program.

6. Stored in an airtight container, the ice cream keeps in the freezer for 5 days.

Per serving: Calories: 152; Total fat: 4g; Saturated fat: 3g; Cholesterol: 16mg; Sodium: 135mg; Carbohydrates: 23g; Fiber: 1g; Protein: 6g

Mango Sorbet

I love the combination of tropical flavors in this dairy-free, fruit-based dessert! Made from only four simple ingredients, this Mango Sorbet is easy to whip up and is totally guilt-free. Don't like mango? No problem. Swap out the frozen mango for any frozen fruit you want. Try raspberries, strawberries, peaches, or pineapple! I also like to top it off with fresh blueberries, shredded coconut and granola for a refreshing morning smoothie bowl.

DAIRY-FREE, GLUTEN-FREE, NUT-FREE, VEGAN, UNDER 30 MINUTES, 5-INGREDIENT

PREP TIME: 5 minutes
BLEND TIME: 1 minute

4 cups frozen mango chunks

1 cup canned full-fat coconut milk

1 tablespoon lime juice

2 tablespoons agave syrup

1. Place the mango, coconut milk, lime juice, and agave syrup into the blender pitcher in the order listed.

2. Select ICE CREAM. Use the tamper to push the ingredients down toward the blades as needed during the program.

3. Stored in an airtight container, the ice cream keeps in the freezer for 5 days.

Per serving: *Calories: 249; Total fat: 12g; Saturated fat: 11g; Cholesterol: 0mg; Sodium: 11mg; Carbohydrates: 38g; Fiber: 3g; Protein: 2g*

Mango Yogurt Ice Pops

SERVES 8

There are so many frozen dessert options these days, but there is something inherently nostalgic about an ice pop—and what is more fun than a homemade ice pop? All you need are some ice pop molds and sticks and you can make this yummy version, which features sweet, creamy mangos, coconut milk, agave syrup, and Greek yogurt. I truly believe these ice pops are the perfect summertime treat, the kind you can eat to cool off on a hot summer afternoon while pretending you are in a tropical paradise.

GLUTEN-FREE, NUT-FREE, VEGETARIAN, 5-INGREDIENT

PREP TIME: 10 minutes
BLEND TIME: 1 minute
CHILL TIME: 3 or 4 hours

HACK IT: If the mango mixture or Greek yogurt is too thick to evenly pour into the ice pop molds, add more coconut milk or a splash of water to thin out the mixture or the yogurt.

2½ cups frozen mango
¾ cup full-fat coconut milk
1 tablespoon agave syrup
1 cup Greek yogurt

1. Place the mango, coconut milk, and agave syrup into the blender pitcher in the order listed.

2. Select ICE CREAM. Use the tamper to push the ingredients down toward the blades as needed during the program.

3. Pour the mango mixture into 8 ice pop molds, until they are each about ⅓ full. Place the ice pop molds in the freezer for 30 minutes.

4. Remove the ice pops from the freezer and add a layer of Greek yogurt to each, filling another ⅓ of the mold. Place the ice pop molds back into the freezer for 30 minutes.

5. Remove the ice pops from the freezer and add the remaining mango mixture to each mold. Secure the ice pop stick in place and place the ice pop molds back in the freezer for 3 hours, until hard.

Per serving: Calories: 101; Total fat: 6g; Saturated fat: 5g; Cholesterol: 4mg; Sodium: 18mg; Carbohydrates: 13g; Fiber: 1g; Protein: 2g

MEASUREMENT CONVERSIONS

VOLUME EQUIVALENTS (LIQUID)

US Standard	US Standard (ounces)	Metric (approximate)
2 tablespoons	1 fl. oz.	30 mL
¼ cup	2 fl. oz.	60 mL
½ cup	4 fl. oz.	120 mL
1 cup	8 fl. oz.	240 mL
1½ cups	12 fl. oz.	355 mL
2 cups or 1 pint	16 fl. oz.	475 mL
4 cups or 1 quart	32 fl. oz.	1 L
1 gallon	128 fl. oz.	4 L

VOLUME EQUIVALENTS (DRY)

US Standard	Metric (approximate)
⅛ teaspoon	0.5 mL
¼ teaspoon	1 mL
½ teaspoon	2 mL
¾ teaspoon	4 mL
1 teaspoon	5 mL
1 tablespoon	15 mL
¼ cup	59 mL
⅓ cup	79 mL
½ cup	118 mL
⅔ cup	156 mL
¾ cup	177 mL
1 cup	235 mL
2 cups or 1 pint	475 mL
3 cups	700 mL
4 cups or 1 quart	1 L

OVEN TEMPERATURES

Fahrenheit (F)	Celsius (C) (approximate)
250°F	120°C
300°F	150°C
325°F	165°C
350°F	180°C
375°F	190°C
400°F	200°C
425°F	220°C
450°F	230°C

WEIGHT EQUIVALENTS

US Standard	Metric (approximate)
½ ounce	15 g
1 ounce	30 g
2 ounces	60 g
4 ounces	115 g
8 ounces	225 g
12 ounces	340 g
16 ounces or 1 pound	455 g

INDEX

ACKNOWLEDGMENTS

First and foremost, thank you to Julien, my best friend, my faithful taste tester, my cameraman, and my husband. Thank you for supporting me and my crazy ideas, for caffeinating me during long days of recipe testing, and for feeding me during late nights of copywriting.

To my friends and family, thank you for your words of encouragement and for cheering for me throughout this journey. I am so thankful to have each and every one of you in my corner.

To my amazing team at Ninja®: Sam, Corey, Meg, Craig, Chelven, and Caroline, thank you for inspiring me every day. Thank you for supporting my wild ideas, for making me excited to come to work, and for filling the world with flavorful recipes.

To Salwa and my team at Callisto Media, thank you for joining me on this journey and for believing in this product. I am so happy to be working with you again and am proud to be part of the Callisto Media family.

Last but never least, to my readers, thank you for trying my recipes and sharing them with your friends and loved ones. I hope you love the Ninja Foodi™ Blender and these recipes as much as I do!

ABOUT THE AUTHOR

 **KENZIE SWANHART** is a home cook turned food blogger and cookbook author, providing her readers inspiration in and out of the kitchen. With more than 250,000 copies of her cookbooks in print, Kenzie never wavers in her mission: creating and sharing with her readers easy, yet flavorful, recipes made with real ingredients.

As the head of culinary marketing and innovation for Ninja®, a leading kitchen appliance company, Kenzie and her team provide a unique, food-first point of view for the development of new products and recipes to make consumers' lives easier and healthier. You'll also see her serving as the face of Ninja on the leading television home shopping network, where she shares tips, tricks, and recipes for the company's full line of products.

Kenzie lives in Boston with her husband Julien and their dog Charlie.